6 Essential Practices
for Income Investors

6 Essential Practices for Income Investors

Jonathan Craig Sarver

IMPORTANT NOTE:

The opinions expressed in this book are those of the author(s) and are not necessarily those of Wells Fargo Advisors or its affiliates. The material has been prepared or is distributed solely for information purposes and is not a solicitation or an offer to buy any security or instrument or to participate in any trading strategy.

Wells Fargo Advisors, LLC, Member SIPC, is a registered broker-dealer and a separate non-bank affiliate of Wells Fargo & Company. CAR 0215-02427

About the Author

Jonathan Sarver earned a law degree from *Seton Hall University School of Law* and graduated *Boston University* with *cum laude* honors. Jonathan has been helping investors for over 18 years. Currently, he works as a First Vice President – Investment Officer for Wells Fargo Advisors, LLC in Mission Woods, Kansas. He primarily helps engineers, corporate executives, business owners, and doctors with their investments.

He resides in a condo in downtown Kansas City near the Sprint Center and the Power and Light District. In his free time he enjoys skiing, cooking, and travel.

Table of Contents

Introduction

Why focus an entire book on the subject of Income Investing? Whether working or retired, many individuals are looking to replace, enhance, or grow their monthly income, with their objective set at not running out of money. Typically, income investors are looking for 1) a steady stream of retirement income, 2) a supplement to investment, wage, or earned income, or 3) an investment aimed at smoothing some of the volatility in their portfolio.

The market drawdown was approximately 48% from September 1st 2000 to October 9th 2002, and the market decline of October 9th 2007 to March 9th 2009 was approximately 55% (Carlisle, 2014)! Other significant "intra-year" stock market drawdowns, that exceed 10%, that occurred since the two cited above include: -15.99% in 2010, -19.39% in 2011, and -12.35% in 2015 (Short, 2015). While there are investors who are curious about the variety of different ways to turn all or part of their asset base into an income stream, in my opinion, there are relatively few books that cover the broad spectrum of "income investing."

With 20% to 30% of individual high-net-worth investors' funds allocated to cash, it appears that investors are facing a dilemma: fearful to commit cash to the stock market, yet unwilling to lock it in low yielding CDs for fear of not keeping up with inflation (Frank, 2014). A recent *BlackRock* survey also supports the picture of an unusually high allocation of investors' net worth to cash (Zulz, October 26th 2015). Specifically, the survey found that investors in the United States have 65% of their net worth in cash (Zulz, October 26th 2015). If one invested $100.00 in the S&P 500 benchmark index{S&P 500 Index (SPX) – Arguably the most widely followed and well known benchmark for tracking large US publicly traded companies. The index is comprised of 500 stocks and represents about 80% of the value of all large capitalization stocks. This is the index that is most often used as a proxy for "the market" or the "US stock market" (http://us.spindices.com/indices/equity/sp-500, 2015).} in 1999, by October 2009, he or she would need future appreciation of 72% to breakeven, after adjusting for inflation (Merrell, 2014). Historically the market has trended in cycles of about 14 years, having ups and downs during the trend, but clearly defining a bull market uptrend or bear market down trend (Easterling, 2015). From 1982 to 2000, the market was in a strong uptrend or "bull market" period. In the decade from 2000 to 2010, the market return became stagnant, with the market in a downtrend or "bear market." For investors who want to live off their savings, living solely off of the growth of their assets may not be a viable option. It makes sense for retired investors to have a focus on income investing.

Often retired investors are used to investing with a growth focus, because they built their retirement assets by investing mostly in stocks in order to outperform inflation and build their asset base. With monthly contributions, and often company matching and profit sharing contributions, the balances of these accounts appeared to grow, or hold up well, even when the stock market had lackluster performance. In addition, those investors who have a 401(k) are typically contributing every year, like clockwork, to their account, and therefore tend to *dollar cost average*, or continue to buy into the stock and bond markets at different intervals, including both market peaks and troughs. This type of consistent investing, regardless of market conditions, tends to prevent the issue of an investor who seeks to time the market, and allows investors to have more of a focus on the goal of wealth accumulation. A periodic investment plan such as dollar cost averaging does not assure a profit or protect against a loss in declining markets. Since such a strategy involves continuous investment, the investor should consider his or her ability to continue purchases through periods of low price levels. However, with the shift in the retirement phase from contributions to distributions, investors may need to shift their focus from capital appreciation to income generation. If an investor takes $50,000.00 a year from their $1,000,000.00 retirement account, and it goes down 10% in the first year, they now have $850,000.00, and now the distribution ratio is high, at 5.88%($50,000.00 / $850,000.00 = 5.88%). A common rule of thumb about distribution rate had been, in the past, that a rate of 4% was considered 'reasonable."

Therefore, in considering an income approach, an investor may be able to create a steady income flow for the purpose of minimizing the possibility of having to take out principal during market downdrafts, which would, potentially compromise their future income stream. Often investors who are still in the workforce will have a growth focus in their retirement account, and then keep large sums of cash and cash alternatives in their non-retirement or taxable accounts. However, in the current low interest rate environment, cash and cash alternatives can have a hard time keeping up with inflation, and may do little to enhance one's monthly income. This book will serve as a basic education on bonds, stocks, annuities, and other income strategies, as well as the different investment structures or vehicles to invest in them. In addition, investment risk, risk measurement, and risk management will be covered as well. Finally, a series of hypothetical case studies are included to bring to life many of the different concepts, and how they apply to income investors with different goals, and income investors with different risk tolerances.

Licensed from www.cartoonstock.com

This book does not constitute advice, and is meant as a starting point on your road to income investing. It is not meant to replace your investment advisor or your own research efforts. In addition, this book does not provide tax or legal advice, and cannot replace the role of your personal attorney, accountant, or tax advisor. It is also important to note that every investor has unique goals, a unique risk tolerance, and a unique financial situation; therefore this book cannot provide the specific customized advice or research an investor needs. Now it is time to get started: as Luke Skywalker of the *Star Wars* films would say if he were an income investor: "May the income be with you!"

I. Practice #1 Utilize Bonds

Polonius: "Neither a borrower, nor a lender be;
For loan oft loses both itself and friend,
And borrowing dulls the edge of husbandry."
SHAKESPEARE: <u>HAMLET</u> ACT *1*, SCENE *3*, *75–77*

What is a bond?

Polonius offered the advice above in Shakespeare's *Hamlet*, warning that when you loan money you can lose both your friend and your money, and that borrowing ruins the virtue of thrift. What is a **bond** anyway? In the simplest terms, a bond is a loan. However, rather than a loan between friends as referred to in the famous quote above, a bond is loan between the issuer (a government, corporation, or municipality), and an investor. The issuer borrows the principal amount for a specified period of time, pays an annual percentage rate of return, or coupon payment, as interest to the investor, and pays back the principal to the investor at the stated date of maturity.

Coupon Payments and Accrued Interest

Bonds are typically issued at $1000.00 *par value* per bond, and can trade above or below the $1,000.00 par amount in the secondary market, based upon changes in a myriad of factors including supply, demand, interest rates, and credit quality. Typically, bonds will pay interest semi-annually in the form of a **coupon payment**. If a bond is sold prior to maturity, the seller is paid all of the interest that has built up between the last coupon payment and the date of sale, and the buyer must pay the seller this **accrued interest** upon purchasing a bond in the secondary market. This way the seller is paid for each and every day that he or she held on to the bond, while the buyer is paid back the accrued interest that he or she pays up front when the next coupon payment is made.

The Secondary Market: Current Yield, Yield to Maturity, and Yield to Call

Bonds can trade above or below par value on what is referred to as the *secondary market*. This market allows investors to buy and sell bonds after a bond is issued.

How can investors compare bonds in the secondary market to ensure they are making smart choices differentiating bond yields? Let's look at an example of a corporate bond issued by XYZ, Incorporated. In this scenario, XYZ, Inc. issues a bond at $1,000.00 face value. Also assume that the bond issue matures in ten years, and pays a 3% coupon, which is $30.00 annually per bond. Therefore the XYZ, Inc. bond is issued with a **nominal yield** or coupon rate of 3% that is constant throughout the ten-year term of the bond (Hallman & Rosenbloom, 2015, p.90).

Let's assume interest rates rise, and this particular XYZ, Inc. bond issue declines in value to $900.00 on the secondary market as a result. Now that the market price of the bond has declined, the current yield is now higher than the nominal yield. The **current yield** is now calculated as follows: $30.00 coupon amount (because the coupon dollar amount remains constant)/$900.00 (the current market value of the bond) = a *current yield* of 3.33% (Hallman & Rosenbloom, 2015 pp. 90-91).

Since the bond will eventually mature at the par value of $1,000.00, the **yield to maturity**, which includes the added amount of the *price appreciation of the bond* from $900.00 to $1,000.00, is even higher than the *current yield* (Hallman & Rosenbloom, 2015, p.91). The formula for calculating yield to maturity is as follows:

Yield to Maturity = (Coupon + Prorated Discount)/([Face Value + Purchase Price]/2).

Prorated Discount = Discount relative to par/number of years to maturity.

Or

Yield to Maturity= (Coupon – Prorated Premium)/((Face Value + Purchase Price)/2).

Prorated Premium= Premium relative to par/number of years to maturity.

In this case, the prorated discount is $100.00/10 years to maturity = $10.00. Now we can solve for yield to maturity: ($30.00 +$10.00)/ (($1,000.00+$900.00)/2) = a 4.21% *yield to maturity* (Hallman & Rosenbloom, 2015, p. 91).

What are a few methods that an investor can employ to make "apples to apples" comparisons of bonds on the secondary market? Assuming the credit quality and the maturity dates of two bonds are identical, investors may want to look to the *yield to maturity* to make an apples to apples comparison of bonds, and select which bonds are more appropriate given their individual situation. Sometimes bonds are **callable bonds**, meaning that an issuer can call the bond for redemption early, typically at par value. It is important for investors to consider this possibility if the bond is callable by looking at the *yield to call*, when comparing bonds on a *yield to maturity* basis.

Different Types of Bonds

While many investors view bonds as a boring "plain vanilla" type of investment, there are multiple types of bonds, including Government Bonds, Mortgage Backed Bonds, Foreign Bonds, Convertible Bonds, Investment Grade Corporate Bonds, High Yield Bonds, Municipal Bonds, and Floating Rate Bonds. While some bonds are more interest rate sensitive, and can gain or lose value based upon interest rate movements, others are more economically sensitive or credit sensitive, and often rise and fall with changes in the economic cycle.

Risks Bond Investors Face

Risk is inherent to the investment landscape. It is a term used to describe the degree of uncertainty and/or of financial loss inherent in an investment or decision. Like any other investment, investments in fixed income products are still subject to risks regardless of the public's tendency to perceive these securities as "safe." Yields and market value will fluctuate so that your investment may be worth less than original cost upon sale, redemption or maturity. There are many different risks faced by bond investors, including:

- **Call risk**—The risk that declining interest rates may accelerate the redemption of a callable security, causing an investor's principal to be returned sooner than expected. As a consequence, investors may suffer from "reinvestment risk", or have to reinvest their principal at a lower rate of interest.
- **Credit risk**—The risk that the issuer of the bonds will be unable to make debt service payments due to a weakening of their credit.
- **Event risk**—The risk that an issuer's ability to make debt service payments will change because of unanticipated changes, such as a corporate restructuring, a regulatory change or an accident, in their environment.
- **Interest rate or market risk**—Potential price fluctuations in a bond due to changes in the general level of interest rates.
- **Underwriting risk**—The risk of pricing and underwriting securities and then ultimately not being able to sell them to the investor.

Let's first focus on these three primary risks: interest rate risk, credit risk, and reinvestment risk.

Interest Rate Risk. One of the most commonly cited risks by the media for bonds is interest rate risk. **Interest rate risk** is the risk that interest rates are going to rise, so that the bond that an investor bought in the past is paying less than the coupon on the newly issued bond from the same issuer, or one of similar credit quality, maturing at the same time. Therefore, the bond the investor purchased in the past will go down in value until the current yield matches the higher yield that bonds from the same issuer, or one of similar credit quality, maturing on the same date, are being issued at currently. An investor who needs to liquidate his bond prior to maturity can lose principal value due to interest rate risk.

In general, bonds that are considered "long term" (maturities greater than 10 years) tend to be the most interest rate sensitive, while intermediate term bonds (maturities from 4 to 10 years) are less interest rate sensitive, and short-term bonds (maturities from one to three years) are comparatively less sensitive to rising rates.

Duration: A measure of interest rate risk. Often bond investors fear inflation, which causes rising interest rates, and in turn can cause bond prices to decline. The longer the term of a bond, the more interest rate sensitive it can be. In addition, the higher the credit quality of a bond, the more interest rate sensitive it is (Pavia, 2014). **Duration** is a metric that bond investors use to measure the effect that each 1% change in interest rates has on a bond's market value. Duration takes into account a bond's interest payments in measuring bond price volatility and is stated in terms of "years." For example a duration of "4," or four years, means that if interest rates were to rise 1%, the bond or bond portfolio would in theory decline by 4%.   Ultimately, the duration of a bond is a measure of its price sensitivity to interest rates, based on the average time to maturity of its interest and principal cash flows. Duration can assist investors in deriving a comparison of bonds with different maturities and coupon rates. While investors may seek to create a low duration portfolio to help mitigate some of the interest rate risk and inflation risk associated with bond portfolios, there are times when a high duration portfolio can be advantageous, such as when interest rates are declining, and investors can take advantage of long-term, investment grade bonds appreciating as interest rates decline.

Credit Risk. Another risk that bond investors face is credit risk. **Credit risk** is the risk that an issuer will miss a coupon payment, default on the bond issue, go out of business, and never pay back the principal, or have their credit rating cut to a lower grade. S&P, Moody's, and Fitch are some of the more widely followed credit rating agencies that rate bond issues for credit quality. Their ratings are intended to express relative opinions about the creditworthiness of an issuer or credit quality of an individual debt issue, from strongest to weakest, within a universe of credit risk. For example, the rating service Standard and Poors or S&P provides ratings on both investment grade and non-investment grade bonds. S&P will assign a rating of AAA, AA, A, or BBB to investment grade bonds, listed from the highest investment grade credit quality to the lowest investment grade credit quality. Non-investment grade bonds will be assigned a rating of BB, B, CCC, CC, C, or D, from the highest non-investment grade credit quality to the lowest non-investment grade credit quality for the Standard and Poors or S&P credit rating service. It is also important to note that rating from "AA" to "CCC" may be modified by the addition of a plus (+) or minus (-) sign to show relative standing within the major rating categories for the S&P or the Standard and Poors credit rating service. Bonds rated BBB- and higher are considered by S&P to be "investment grade," which are less likely to default. Bonds rated lower than BBB-, or BB+ and lower, are considered non-investment or speculative grade debt, and are considered to have a greater probability of default than investment grade bonds.

Reinvestment Risk. The final major risk that we will discuss here that a bond investor may face is reinvestment risk. **Reinvestment risk** is the risk that interest income or principal repayments will have to be reinvested at a lower rate of return. In the post-2009 financial crisis investment landscape, many investors have faced the dilemma of reinvestment risk. Consider this hypothetical example. Imagine an investor purchased a long-term fixed income product with a coupon rate of 5% prior to the crisis. Now, let's imagine that this product matured in 2015 and the investor was faced with two challenges – reinvesting the principal and interest at an interest rate of 3.3% (the rate of the Bloomberg US Corporate Bond Index as of October 15th 2015) which is significantly lower than when they made their initial investment (www.bloomberg.com, 2015, markets/rates + bonds/ United States / Bloomberg US Corporate Bond Index). As you can imagine, it can be difficult to recreate the income stream needed when interest rates have declined significantly!

I. A. Convertible Bonds

2nd Witch: "Eye of newt, and toe of frog,
Wool of bat, and tongue of dog,
Adder's fork, and blind-worm's sting,
Lizard's leg, and howlet's wing,
For a charm of powerful trouble,
Like a hell-broth boil and bubble."
SHAKESPEARE: <u>MACBETH</u> ACT 4, SCENE 1, 14-15

While a **convertible bond** may not be as strange and fangled as a witches brew, it is a hybrid security with both fixed income and equity-like characteristics (Spiegeleer, Schoutens, & Van Hulle, 2014, p. 19). A convertible bond is a bond that gives the holder the option – but not the obligation – to convert the bond to the underlying issuer's stock at a specified price or "conversion ratio," prior to the maturity of the bond (Spiegeleer, Schoutens, & Van Hulle, 2014, pp. 5-6). Below is an example of a hypothetical XYZ, Inc. corporate bond issue and a hypothetical XYZ, Inc. convertible bond issue:

Example 1: Corporate Bond. XYZ, Inc. issues a speculative grade corporate bond that carries a 5% coupon and matures in ten years. This is fairly straightforward. The investor "loans" XYZ, Inc. $10,000.00 for 10 bonds, which are issued in $1,000.00 lots. In return, XYZ, Inc. pays the investor 5% per year in interest, which is usually paid in semi-annual installments, in this case $250.00 every six months. At maturity, in ten years, the investor receives his or her money or principal back from XYZ, Inc., in this case $10,000.00.

Example 2: Convertible Bond. XYZ, Inc. issues a speculative grade convertible bond that carries a 4% coupon and matures in ten years. In addition, the XYZ, Inc. convertible bond comes with an embedded option, where the investor has the right to convert each $1,000.00 bond into 8 shares of XYZ, Inc. stock, and XYZ, Inc. is priced at $100 per share at the time this convertible is publicly issued or sold to investors as a new issue. XYZ, Inc. is happy to be able to pay a lower coupon rate of 4% for their convertible issue than the 5% coupon their regular corporate bond is paying. The investor accepts this lower coupon rate of 4%, rather than the 5% the regular corporate bond is paying, in exchange for the right to convert this bond into XYZ common stock. The 1 percentage point lower coupon rate is reflective of the cost of the embedded conversion feature of the convertible bond. The gap between the $1,000.00 par value of the convertible bond and the $800.00 initial conversion value is known as the **conversion premium,** or the amount by which the price of the convertible security exceeds the current market value of the stock to which it may be converted (Bank, 2015).

In a way, convertible bonds provide investors with a security that combines the characteristics of traditional fixed income products as well as the potential for capital appreciation most associated with common stock (Spiegeleer, Schoutens, & Van Hulle, 2014, pp. 5,19,22-23). In this hypothetical example, let's imagine that XYZ, Inc. is speculative grade or high yield rated BB+ or lower by S&P. When a convertible's underlying common stock moves higher, the conversion privilege becomes more valuable. This may cause a rise in the price of the convertible bond, too. Now what if XYZ, Inc. began consistently missing earnings by a significant margin, it has an accounting scandal, or a key employee leaves the company for a competitor? Any of these events could cause a sharp drop in the price of XYZ, Inc. stock, and in turn, have a negative impact upon the price of the XYZ, Inc. convertible bond. What if XYZ, Inc. stock went down 50% from $100.00 per share to $50.00 per share? How would this impact the price of the convertible bond? The answer is that - if the company's stock declines to a price that makes the convertible feature worthless but they continue to make principal and interest payments – the convertible security will trade solely on its value as a fixed income instrument.

This point at which the convertible option is being priced as worthless because the underlying stock price has fallen is called the "bond floor."

In this case, the XYZ, Inc. 10 year convertible bond will hit its bond floor at $800.00. The math to solve for the bond floor is as follows: 4% of the $1,000.00 face value of the XYZ, Inc. 10 year convertible bond (the coupon payment) is $40.00. Now $40.00 / X (what decreased principle amount) = 5% (which is the coupon payment or rate of interest of the speculative grade XYZ, Inc. ten year straight bond). The equation to solve for the bond floor is $40/X=5%. This establishes the bond floor at $800.00.

It is important to note that while the bond floor provides a certain level of safety and stability of price, once the convertible hits the level of the bond floor, it will move in tandem with the straight bond, both up and down in value. It should also be noted that convertibles have historically been more volatile than bonds, but not as volatile as stocks (Spiegeleer, Schoutens, & Van Hulle, 2014 p.20).

As one can see from the XYZ, Inc. convertible bond example above, convertibles provide potential capital appreciation, similar to common stocks; yet provide the stability and income that investors typically associate with corporate bonds. While a stock can drop sharply as a result of a lackluster earnings report, the underlying corporate issuer of a convertible bond must just demonstrate viability, and stability of credit quality, for the price of a convertible to maintain the level of its bond floor. In addition, assuming the corporate issuer does not default or go bankrupt, the convertible investor will receive the full $1,000.00 face value at the maturity date. Investors who seek current income while having the potential for capital appreciation may want to consider these investments as part of their asset allocation strategy.

I. B. High-Yield Bonds

"During a company's innovation and growth phase, it's
natural for its debt to be rated below-investment-grade.
Many of America's largest corporations started out as
high-yield firms. Even the United States of America
had to issue high-yield debt in its early years, when
Alexander Hamilton was Secretary of the Treasury."

MICHAEL MILKEN (MIKEMILKEN.COM,

QUOTES, HIGH-YIELD BONDS)

Most investors understand, or find out the hard way, that the greater the potential return, or yield of an asset, all else being equal, the greater risk an investor assumes. The additional return a particular asset class achieves over time, over the "risk free rate" (a theoretical rate of return of an investment that presents no risk of financial loss), as a result of assuming a greater level or risk, is called the **risk premium**. For example, long-term bonds may pay a higher interest rate, as a "risk premium," because the investor has a greater degree of uncertainty as to changes in interest rates and credit quality over a long period of time. Similarly, *speculative grade debt* investors are rewarded with a risk premium and are paid a higher rate of annual interest than investors in *investment grade debt*.

High-yield bonds, or speculative debt, affectionately known as "junk bonds," are bonds that are rated less than investment grade, less than BBB- by S&P or BB by Fitch's. While high yield bonds pay a greater rate of interest than their investment grade neighbors in the bond universe, they carry a greater degree of credit risk as well. **Credit risk** is the risk that a corporate, municipal, or government issuer of bonds will default on an interest or coupon payment, or the credit quality of the issuer will deteriorate and rating agencies will cut the credit rating of the issuer, or the company will go bankrupt or out of business.

Why in the world would anyone want to own risky bonds? Aren't investors drawn to bonds for their perceived safety compared to stocks? Investors in speculative grade debt are typically rewarded with a higher annual interest rate than investment grade debt. Small and medium size businesses and new businesses may not have the financial strength and history to garner an investment grade rating, yet as Michael Milken, the infamous junk bond king, alluded to above, these newer companies may eventually be the large investment-grade companies of tomorrow. Keep in mind that, while an investment-grade company may be considered "safer" than a speculative-grade company today, the higher credit quality bond's credit quality can potentially deteriorate, while the lower quality bond's credit quality could potentially improve. Therefore it is important when considering both investment grade and speculative grade debt to make buy and sell decisions based upon your goals, objectives and appetite for risk.

The Economic Cycle and High Yield Bonds

The overall economy can impact speculative grade bond investors. As the economy improves, small and medium size companies, which tend to be the largest issuers of speculative grade debt, may perform better with an advancing economy. This can also be true of small capitalization stocks as well.

High-yield debt appreciation hypothetical example: A.B. Clothes ("ABC") is a teen and young adult casual clothing retailer that had trouble attracting non-essential purchases during the "Great Recession" from 2007 through 2009. During the depths of the credit crises, ABC had to pay a 10% annual coupon rate in order to issue new ten-year bonds. However, in 2015 credit sensitive bonds have recovered significantly in price since the "Great Recession" with the overall economy. Now ABC, while still garnering a junk or speculative grade debt rating, has an improved financial outlook, just as people feel more confident to spend on non-essential items now that the Great Recession is over.

Therefore, ABC decides to issue new corporate debt with a 6% coupon that is due at the same time as the old 2007 debt. This debt, issued at 10% during the credit crises, will now appreciate in value from $1,000.00 to $1,666.66, bringing the yield on the debt to 6%, in order to match where the new debt is being priced. We can solve for the increased principal amount as follows: First, the coupon yield of the $1,000.00 2007 ABC bond is 10% or $100.00. Second, the coupon yield of today's ABC bonds is 6%. Thus, the equation to determine the increased principal amount for the ABC debt issued in 2007 is $100.00/X=6%, establishing the increased principle amount as $1,666.66. Now let's take a look at the opposite hypothetical scenario:

High-yield debt hypothetical loss of principal example: Of course the economy could fall into another recession. If a recession were to occur now, ABC being a cyclical retailing stock could possibly be affected by an economic downturn and trigger a loss in the principal amount of ABC bonds. Assume that high unemployment, poor consumer confidence, the European debt situation, and slow domestic growth force the United States back into a recession. Under that scenario, newly issued ABC bonds, maturing at the same time as the old ABC bonds issued in 2015 with a 6% coupon, could price with a 10% coupon yield. This would cause the older 2015 ABC bond issuance with a 6% coupon to sink in price to a *decreased principal amount* of $600.00, pushing the yield up to 10% to match where the new issuance of ABC debt is trading. In this case, the *decreased principal amount* would be $60.00/X=10% or $600.00.

High-yield bonds can provide income and potential for price appreciation during times of growing GDP and economic expansion. However, speculative grade debt can cause loss of principal and portfolio declines in times of recession and contracting GDP. Historically, the average **yield spread**, or credit spread, or differential between junk bonds and treasuries of a similar maturity has been approximately 6% (Aneiro, 2014). In times of excess, like right before the credit crises started to hit in the summer of 2007, the spread between junk bonds and treasuries was less than 3%, while at the height of the credit crises the spread ballooned to over 21% (Aneiro, 2014). With many high quality government (10 year US Treasury Yield of 2.01% as of October 15th 2015) and corporate bonds { Bloomberg US Corporate Bond Index: A diversified bond index created by Bloomberg for the purpose of creating a benchmark for tracking the changes in value and yield of United States investment grade corporate bonds. As of October 29, 2015, the index had the following relevant characteristics: "yield to maturity" of 3.37%, "effective duration" of 7.04, "average life" of 10.49, and the number of issues that comprise the diversified index is 5,543.

(http://www.bloomberg.com/quote/BUSC:IND, 2015)} yielding approximately 2% to approximately 3% today, high-yield bonds can potentially be an attractive alternative for income and potential appreciation for part of an investor's bond portfolio (www.bloomberg.com, 2015, markets/rates + bonds/United States/ US Treasury Yields/ 10 year, markets/rates + bonds/US bonds/Bloomberg US Corporate Bond Index). Of course, investors should not place undue reliance on yield as a factor to be considered in selecting bond investments. The appropriate amount of exposure to high yield bonds is different for each investor, depending upon economic conditions, market conditions, and one's personal risk tolerance and goals.

I. C. Municipal Bonds

"Everything appears to promise that it will last; but nothing in this world is certain but death and taxes."

BENJAMIN FRANKLIN

Maybe **municipal bonds** were created after Ben Franklin's time, because they are bonds issued by specific states, local municipalities, counties, and US territories that are free from federal, state and local taxes. Since the bonds pay interest not subject to tax, they typically have *lower coupon rates than corporate taxable bonds* of the same credit quality that mature in the same year. Historically, municipal bonds on average have yielded 80% of the yield of US treasuries (Hallman & Rosenbloom, 2015, p.144). This rule of thumb can be used as a benchmark to gauge whether municipal bonds are undervalued or overvalued. Municipal bonds are somewhat more credit sensitive than interest rate sensitive. Investors could buy municipal bonds with longer maturity dates and higher credit quality than the corporate bonds they buy. Since the "taxable equivalent yield" of municipal bonds is often significantly higher than taxable corporate bonds of the same credit quality, maturing at the same time, municipal bonds are somewhat insulated from interest rate risk. Many municipal issues are rated AA and AAA, so much so that portfolios or funds of municipal securities rated A to BBB- for average credit quality are often considered high-yield or high-income municipal bond investments, even though they still have an average credit quality of investment grade. While many strategists have questioned the credit quality of municipal bonds, the historical default rate has been low. In 2014 .17% of the deals that S&P Dow Jones follows were in default (Slavin, 2015).

General Obligation Bonds vs. Revenue Bonds

A **general obligation bond** is a municipal bond issued by a state or local government that is backed by the taxing power of the issuing entity (Hallman & Rosenbloom, 2015, p. 144). While in *general*, no pun intended, states have greater latitude to increase taxes than cities do, defaults are highly uncommon among *general obligation* bonds (Hallman & Rosenbloom, 2015, p. 144). A **revenue bond** is a municipal bond issued by a government authority to fund a public work, such as a university building, toll road, bridge, medical facility, or basic utility, such as sewer, water, and electricity (Hallman & Rosenbloom, 2015, p. 144). Since these bonds are backed by the revenues, tolls, and fees of the public work, and not directly by the state or city, they are considered riskier, and typically pay a higher rate of interest (Hallman & Rosenbloom, 2015, p. 144).

Low Correlation

In addition to the fact that municipal bonds are typically not subject to federal income taxation, municipal bonds provide a way to invest in bonds that have a very low correlation to stocks. Historically, municipal bonds have been considered to be a good hedge for stock investors, because they tend to move more like treasuries, and appreciate in value when there is a "flight to quality," or a recession, yet are still considered a spread product, because their taxable equivalent yield is usually higher, or at a spread greater than a comparable Treasury. According to Dr. Harry Markowitz, the father of **Modern Portfolio Theory**, investing in a portfolio of non-correlated assets, or assets that move independently of one another – both when advancing and declining – tends to reduce overall portfolio risk and improve returns.

Taxable Equivalent Yield

Often investors must make a choice between a corporate bond issue and a municipal issue of the same credit quality maturing at the same time. Without thinking, a novice investor may choose the corporate issue because the coupon is a higher annual interest payment, not taking into account the *taxable equivalent yield* of the municipal bond. The **taxable equivalent yield** is the metric by which an investor can make an "apples to apples" comparison between a tax free municipal bond issue and a taxable bond of the same maturity date, figuring *what would a taxable bond have to yield*, for it to have an equivalent yield to the municipal bond *after federal and state taxes are taken into account*.

Taxable equivalent yield hypothetical example. A 2015 Jackson County, Missouri Unified School District 5 year bond with a 1.25% coupon is state and federally tax exempt for Missouri residents (www.bloomberg.com, October 15, 2015, markets/rates + bonds/ United States/ US Municipal Bonds/ Muni Bonds 5 year yield = 1.22%). {BVAL Municipal Benchmark 5 Year Index: A diversified US tax exempt AAA (average credit quality from Moody's and S&P) municipal bond index created by Bloomberg for the purpose of creating a benchmark for tracking the changes in value and yield of 5 year municipal bonds. Bloomberg uses data from the Municipal Securities Rulemaking Board, new issue calendars, and other proprietary sources. (http://www.bloomberg.com/quote/ BVMB5Y:IND, 2015)} A retired Missouri school teacher, affection- ately called Mrs. Old School, living in Kansas City, MO wants to sup- port the local schools, but isn't sure that 1.25% makes sense, because she can get 2.00% on a 5 year CD from a bank (www.money-rates. com, October 15th, 2015). She is retired, and living off of social secu- rity, a small 403(b) retirement plan, and a small pension, which puts her in the 25% federal tax bracket and 6% MO State tax bracket. She wants to know what the taxable equivalent yield on the 1.25% Missouri municipal bond is. The total tax for Mrs. Old School is added as follows: 25% federal tax + 6% MO State tax = 31% in total tax. Therefore after taxes, Mrs. Old School will only receive 69% of any income generated by a taxable investment, like a CD (100% - 31% = 69%). In order to solve for the taxable equivalent yield that a CD would have to have to be equal to the 1.25% MO municipal bond, the equation is as follows: the taxable equivalent yield is the tax free yield of the municipal bond (in this case 1.25%) divided by the percentage of the taxable investment yield left after taxes are tak- en into account (in this case 69%) = 1.81% taxable equivalent yield. Clearly in this case the 2% CD trumps the MO tax-free municipal bond, and Mrs. Old School should select the bank CD over choos- ing to support the Missouri schools and receive a higher payout even after the tax advantage of the Missouri municipal bond issue is taken into account.

Geography and Municipal Bonds

In general, Mrs. Old School will want to buy Missouri municipal bonds, assuming the rate is attractive relative to other alternatives such as bank CDs, because she lives in Missouri, and therefore will not have to pay any state or federal income taxes on the coupon or interest payments for municipal bonds purchased in her state of legal residence. However, if Mrs. Old School moved to Kansas, she would have to pay KS State income taxes on her MO municipal bond. Therefore, all else being equal, it would make sense for Mrs. Old School to stick to buying bonds in KS after moving there. Some states have no state income tax: Alaska, Florida, Nevada, South Dakota, Texas, Washington and Wyoming (Boitnott, 2015). (Tennessee and New Hampshire don't have to file a return to pay taxes on wages however, dividend and interest income is taxed.) If Mrs. Old School decided to move to Texas to be closer to her children and grandchildren, she could then buy municipal bonds issued by any state, without paying state or federal income tax. Some municipal bond investors, who live in states with a personal income tax, will employ a strategy where they can survey the national municipal bond market in order to find better yields, even after adjusting for the extra tax burden of purchasing out-of-state municipal bonds. Some states, such as Kansas, have a low issuance of municipal bonds, and therefore KS residents will often look nationally for municipal bonds. In addition, municipal issues from Guam, Puerto Rico, and other US territories, are double tax exempt of both state and federal taxes for residents of all 50 US states. While the interest income is tax-free, capital gains, if any, will be subject to taxes. Income for some investors may be subject to the federal Alternative Minimum Tax (AMT).

I. D. Government Securities

Caesar: "I am constant as the northern star,
Of whose true-fix'd and resting quality
There is no fellow in the firmament."
SHAKESPEARE: *JULIUS CAESAR* ACT 3, SCENE 1, 60–62

T he **ten-year US Treasury bond** is the "northern star" of the bond universe, and helps bond investors gauge where the bond market is priced, just like the northern star once provided navigational perspective to travelers (Zeng, 2015). The 3-month Treasury is sometimes referred to as the "risk free rate," because it carries virtually no credit risk, and is backed by the full faith and credit of the United States Treasury. All other bonds price at a spread from treasuries or a margin of interest greater than treasuries, based upon their perceived credit risk. Ironically, while US treasury bonds carry virtually no credit risk, they do carry a great deal of interest rate risk, especially the longer term issues. The longer term a bond is, the greater the interest rate risk is. Also the higher credit quality a bond is, the greater the interest rate risk is (Pavia, 2014). Short-term treasuries, with a term of only a few months, are **treasury bills**. Treasury securities with a term of one to ten years are referred to as **treasury notes**.

Licensed from www.cartoonstock.com

Often investors will buy **zero coupon treasuries**. They pay no coupon or interest payment, are purchased at a deep discount to the $1,000.00 par value, and will mature at par. *Zeroes* tend to be even more interest rate sensitive than coupon paying treasuries, but investors are rewarded for this additional risk with a higher *yield to maturity* associated with *zeroes*. Often investors will **ladder** their zero coupon treasuries, or stagger the maturities, so that some bonds are maturing every year, and when a bond does mature, the investor will buy another bond at the long end of the **bond ladder**. This strategy utilizes short-term bonds to guard against inflation and interest rate risk, and long-term bonds to guard against deflation and reinvestment risk. (Keep in mind, of course, that a bond ladder strategy doesn't guarantee a profit or protect against loss in a declining market.) Often this strategy is employed in tax-deferred accounts, such as IRAs, because *zeros* pay no interest, yet in a taxable account investors have to pay tax each year on the *phantom interest*, based upon the *yield to maturity* of the zero coupon bonds. When considering a purchase of a zero coupon bond, an investor should keep in mind that the market value of zero coupon bonds fluctuates more with changes in market conditions than regular coupon bonds and, therefore, may not be suitable for all investors.

As of October of 2015, the ten year Treasury has a low yield, which implies slow growth and a low inflation rate for the US economy, while if the yield were to go up significantly, it would imply a greater inflation rate, and in turn relatively more rapid growth for the US economy. So with a low interest rate on a ten-year Treasury, why would any investor want to buy one? 1) Some treasury investors are **insurance companies and pension funds** that have to balance risks with compliance with their investment objective, and they need predictable cash flows to back up pension liability, and potential future insurance company liabilities. 2) **Money market funds** also typically carry treasuries along with CDs and other high quality securities. 3) Another buyer of treasuries is an investor who wants to **own treasuries as a hedge** against those assets typically perceived as being "riskier" such as stocks, corporate bonds, high yield bonds, and convertibles. For example, all else being equal, on days where the S&P 500 benchmark stock index drops by a significant 1% or 2% or more, the 10 year Treasury bond will typically appreciate in value. In 2008, when the credit crises prompted a 37% drawdown in the S&P 500 stock index, long term US Government bond funds appreciated by 23%, providing a solid hedge when nearly all other investments declined sharply in value (Benz, 2015).

Government Agency Bonds

A close cousin of a Treasury security is a government agency bond. **Agencies** are government bonds, backed by government departments, government sponsored enterprises, and government entities such as the Tennessee Valley Authority, The Department of Housing and Urban Development, Fannie Mae, and Freddie Mac. Agency securities are popular because they have the implied backing of the US Treasury, but not the direct backing, and therefore are perceived as nearly as safe from a credit standpoint, but pay a higher interest rate.

For similar reasons that they invest in treasuries, pension funds and insurance companies, money market funds, and investors looking for a hedge for their stocks and other assets considered to be riskier may invest in government agency securities.

I. E. Mortgage Backed Securities

"There still aren't any safety seals for
mortgage backed securities."

Boston University economics professor

Laurence Kotlikoff (Rudawsky, 2010)

Mortgage backed securities are bonds that are backed by residential home mortgages, and the principal and interest payments are made by homeowners. Investment banks will take a pool of hundreds of mortgages and securitize them into a bond instrument that can be bought, sold, and traded as one security. These securities are typically bought and sold by institutions, and are often only available for purchase in larger blocks, typically with a minimum of $1,000,000.00. They may not be popular, outside of a mutual fund or privately managed portfolio, for individual investors. Another hurdle for investors in mortgage-backed securities is the fact that often homeowners will refinance their mortgages (due to a better available interest rate), and this will create an accelerated return of principal for investors in mortgage-backed securities. Generally, when interest rates decline, prepayments accelerate beyond the initial pricing assumptions, which could cause the average life and expected maturity of the securities to shorten. Conversely, when interest rates rise, prepayments slow down beyond the initial pricing assumptions, and could cause the average life and expected maturity of the securities to extend, and the market value to decline. Also the prepayment factor makes it difficult to gauge how long term a mortgage backed security really is, and potentially exposes investors to *reinvestment risk*, if the principal is repaid early.

Subprime mortgage backed securities are mortgage backed securities where the homeowners have poor credit histories and are considered to be less than prime borrowers. The credit crises of 2008, where many banks and brokerage firms failed, and the United States economy went into the Great Recession, was caused by banks taking billions of dollars in losses in subprime mortgage backed securities. Relaxed lending standards, questionable credit ratings, a bubble in US housing, and fraud throughout the system, all contributed to the collapse of the subprime mortgage backed security market and the US housing market. While Kotlikoff's quote above characterizes mortgage backed securities as dangerous, a high quality mortgage backed securities portfolio, in a mutual fund or run by a private asset manager, can be a suitable addition to a bond portfolio.

Licensed from www.politicalcartoons.com

I. F. Floating Rate Bank Loans, Floating Rate Bonds, Treasury Inflation Protected Securities

"By a continuing process of inflation, governments can confiscate, secretly and unobserved, an important part of the wealth of their citizens."

JOHN MAYNARD KEYNES

Inflation, or the decrease in purchasing power per unit of currency, is most bond investors' worst enemy. One may recall buying a tank of gas in 1998 for approximately 75 cents a gallon. In October of 2015 the national average was $2.24 a gallon (www.missourigasprices.com). However, for buyers of floating rate and inflation protected bonds, inflation is a friend (voyainvestments. com, 2015). As inflation rises, these inflation-fighting bonds tend to appreciate in value, because their yields rise in tandem with inflation. Often investors will buy some inflation indexed or floating rate securities to hedge a bond portfolio, because the floating rate and inflation indexed bonds will appreciate in a rising interest rate environment, while the traditional fixed rate bonds, have an inverse relationship to interest rates, and will decline in value as rates rise, especially long term high quality bonds.

Floating Rate Bank Loans

One way to combat inflation is a floating rate bank loan. A **floating rate bank loan** is a senior secured loan to a corporate borrower that is backed by collateral, and where the interest rate floats with inflation every 30 to 90 days. The loans typically price off of the three month LIBOR or the London Interbank Offer Rate as published in The Wall Street Journal, Eastern Edition. The LIBOR rate is a standard financial index used by banks in setting rates on many consumer loans. {London Interbank Offered Rate (LIBOR): a common benchmark interest rate that is used by banks and financial institutions to make changes to adjustable rate mortgages, financial instruments, business loans, as well as floating rate lines of credit. The acronym stands for "London Interbank Offered Rate" and is determined by using rates that banks charge each other for short term loans (http://www.bankrate.com/rates/interest-rates/libor.aspx, 2015; http://www.investopedia.com/terms/l/libor.asp, 2015).} The loans are made to high-yield or speculative grade debt corporate borrowers, but the risk associated with floating rate bank loans is less than high yield bonds issued directly from a corporation, because they are senior loans secured by collateral, and will be ahead of other creditors in the case of a default. While recovery rates have averaged approximately 46% for high yield bond defaults from 1995 through December of 2014, senior secured floating rate bank loans have had an average recovery rate of approximately 70% over the same time period (voyainvestments.com, 2015). While the floating rate bank loans are only traded in the institutional marketplace, individuals can access them through mutual funds and closed-end funds (voyainvestments.com, 2015).

Inflation Indexed Bonds

While **inflation indexed bonds**, or floating rate bonds or notes, are not backed by collateral, they are often issued by investment grade rated corporations, and pay a floating coupon rate that resets every 30, 60, or 90 days based upon an inflation benchmark such as LIBOR, the federal funds rate, the Consumer Price Index (CPI) {Consumer Price Index (CPI): This index is a widely followed index used to track inflation in the economy. It tracks monthly figures for prices for a set of goods and services purchased by urban consumers. The index is maintained by the United States Department of Labor Bureau of Labor Statistics. Yields on some inflation indexed bonds, social security payment increases, and retirement contributions are all determined by changes in "CPI" (http://www.bls.gov/

cpi/, 2015).}, or the three month Treasury bill. While credit quality risk is minimal in investment grade floating rate bonds, because of their high credit quality and willingness to pay more as inflation rises, these securities typically pay less than regular fixed rate bonds, and tend to do poorly in a deflationary or falling interest rate environment. While investors often strategically move in and out of floating rate bonds, a popular strategy is to put 5% to 10% of a bond portfolio in inflation indexed bonds as a hedge against rising interest rates.

Treasury Inflation Protected Securities – TIPS

The highest credit quality floating rate bonds are **treasury inflation protected securities**. They are issued in 5-, 10-, and 20-year maturities, and are indexed to the CPI. Both the credit risk and interest rate risk appear to be minimal, since the US Treasury backs them and they float with the CPI. However, similar to other types of floating rate bonds or loans, they can get hit by deflation. Often pension funds, mutual fund managers, and even individuals buying directly from the US Treasury will use TIPS to hedge their exposure to inflation. Also, TIPS prove useful for adding an asset class that doesn't typically correlate closely with traditional fixed rate bonds or stocks. The yield on TIPS is considered to be a **real yield**, or yield after the effect of inflation. Often investors will take the rate on the 10-year treasury (2.09% as of October 9th 2015) and subtract the yield on the 10-year TIPS (.55% as of October 9th 2015) to arrive at the current inflation rate that bond market participants are pricing into the marketplace (1.54% as of October 9th 2015) (www.bloomberg.com, 2015; Zeng, 2015).

II. Practice #2 Consider Annuities

"When a retiree's portfolio suffers a significant drawdown relatively close to retirement, the likelihood of portfolio failure during the retiree's lifetime increases dramatically. That risk can be mitigated substantially by purchasing an income annuity." (SEAWRIGHT, 2013)

A recent survey entitled "Wells Fargo Middle Class Retirement survey" found that 22% of workers indicated they would rather die than run out of money (Kadlec, 2014)! Retirees used to be able to live on pension and social security income alone. However, today there is an ongoing trend of companies ceasing to offer traditional defined benefit pension plans, and employees are now largely responsible for their own retirement through defined contribution plans, such as 401(k) plans, 403(b) plans, 457 plans, Simplified Employee Pension (SEP) IRA plans, Savings Incentive Match Plan for Employees (SIMPLE) IRA plans, and others. Only 24% of the *Fortune* 500 employers provided traditional defined benefit pension plans at the end of 2013 (Marte, 2014). With many employees receiving no guaranteed retirement income from corporate defined benefit pensions, or pensions paying out a fixed monthly income for a lifetime, it is possible that more and more retirees could turn to an income stream from fixed annuities, variable annuities, and single premium immediate annuities to address their income needs.

Licensed from www.cartoonstock.com

II. A. Fixed Annuities

If investors believe that the US is going to suffer a deflationary spiral, similar to Japan's 20-year slide after its real estate bubble burst in the early 90s, then long term fixed annuities may be worth considering as an investment vehicle. An insurance company issues Deferred Fixed Annuities which may (1) guarantee the principal investment to be repaid in full at the maturity date, and (2) guarantee a fixed annual interest payment over the term of the annuity. If investors fear deflation, they may want to lock in a fixed rate for a longer period of time, such as ten years, to help guard against deflation and reinvestment risk. It is important that investors consider that fixed annuities may have a higher initial interest rate which is guaranteed for a limited time period only. At the end of the guarantee period, the contract may renew at a lower rate. Additionally, investors should carefully consider their liquidity and income needs prior to purchasing a fixed annuity, since they are illiquid investments, carrying high surrender charges that may extend for many years. Typically the surrender charge will decline 1% a year until the maturity of the fixed annuity. Also, withdrawals of any earnings are subject to ordinary income tax. If the investor does not take the income stream, the interest is tax deferred and accumulates in the account. In addition, fixed annuities do not change in value on an investor's statement, which may be important for "psychological" reasons. While other investments may fluctuate based on news, interest rates or other factors, fixed annuities do not depreciate in price and maintain their principal value, regardless of rising interest rates as the principal, interest rate and the periodic payment schedule is outlined in the annuity contract. Additionally, all earnings compound tax deferred and – upon death of the annuitant – the policy proceeds go directly to the named beneficiary, bypassing probate.

II. B. Single Premium Immediate Annuities

W hat if you thought your heirs would squander their newly found wealth on speedboats, yachts, and sports cars? What if you also cared more about living on a guaranteed income during your own lifetime, rather than leaving behind an asset at all? If you are an investor with these concerns, than a single premium immediate annuity (SPIA) may be an investment vehicle to consider. A single premium immediate annuity is an agreement with an insurance company where the investor provides a lump sum of money up front, in a single premium, and in turn receives a fixed annual rate payment from the insurance company for the rest of his or her life, forfeiting the asset up front for this lifetime guaranteed payment stream. A SPIA can be appealing to investors who have no heirs, or no goal of passing wealth to the next generation(s), and would like a guaranteed retirement income stream that is not directly affected by what happens in the financial markets. Similar to a fixed annuity, a SPIA solves the potential problem of having to reinvest at lower rates in the future, or reinvestment risk, and a SPIA also can help address an investors concerns with deflation. However, fixed annuity investors and SPIA investors suffer if inflation sets in, because then their fixed monthly payments will be able to buy fewer and fewer goods as purchasing power is eroded by inflation.

II. C. Variable Annuities

A variable annuity is a contract between a person and an insurance company, where an investor invests a lump sum (alternatively, they may opt to make a series of deposits) with an insurance company, and has a choice to invest in a broad universe of different asset classes in the variable annuity through different *sub accounts*.

A Spectrum of Death Benefits

While many of today's variable annuity investors are more focused on the *income benefit value* and the guaranteed lifetime income during retirement, which will be discussed below, for some investors the *death benefit* is the benefit of primary importance. While each variable annuity insurance contract is different, and offers different variations of death benefits as standard or a rider, we will discuss the basic death benefits offered.

A common feature of variable annuities is the death benefit. If you die, the person that you have selected as a beneficiary will receive the greater of all money in the variable annuity account or some guaranteed minimum.

One of the most simple and straightforward death benefit options is the *dollar for dollar death benefit*. This provides a death benefit for an annuity investor's heirs of the initial premium minus any withdrawals taken. For example, imagine an investor were to invest $100,000.00 in a Variable Annuity contract and take out $10,000.00 in withdrawals prior to his or her death. Let's say that the annuitant dies and the contract was worth $80,000.00 at the time of death, the heirs would receive a higher amount because the *dollar for dollar death benefit* would be $90,000.00.

Another common death benefit is the *pro-rata death benefit*. Under the *pro-rata death benefit*, the initial contract value is reduced by a percentage amount equal to the total of his or her withdrawals divided by the reduced contract value on the date of death. Assume an investor invested $100,000.00 in a Variable Annuity contract. Now assume he or she took out $10,000.00 prior to his or her death, and the contract value also reduced to $50,000.00 over the same period. $10,000.00 of withdrawals is 20% of the $50,000.00 reduced contract value, and therefore under the *pro-rata death benefit*, the initial

$100,000.00 contract value is reduced by 20% for an $80,000.00 death benefit.

Some variable annuities will allow an investor to choose a death benefit rider, for an additional cost, that "steps up". Under this feature, your guaranteed minimum death benefit may be based on a greater amount than purchase payments minus withdrawals. For example, the guaranteed minimum might be your account value as of a specified date, which may be greater than purchase payments minus withdrawals if the underlying investment options have performed well. The purpose of a stepped-up death benefit rider is to "lock in" your investment performance and prevent a later decline in the value of your account from eroding the amount that you expect to leave to your heirs. This feature carries a charge, however, which will reduce your account value. Variable annuities sometimes offer other optional features and riders, which also have extra charges. One common feature, the guaranteed minimum income benefit, guarantees a particular minimum level of annuity payments, even if you do not have enough money in your account (perhaps because of investment losses) to support that level of payments. Other features may include long-term care insurance, which pays for home health care or nursing home care if you become seriously ill.

Income Benefit Value for the Purpose of Taking Guaranteed Lifetime Income

How many investors know what their stocks, bonds, and other investments will be worth the day they choose to retire? What do annuity investors attempt to do when they want to grow their money for the purpose of taking an income stream in retirement at a later date down the road, but they don't want to take on the *systemic risk* that the *amount from which they will take future distributions* will be diminished by poor timing, or retiring, or taking income during a stock, or bond market decline? They add an **income benefit value** rider!

While it holds no cash value, an **income benefit value** rider allows investors to grow the *amount from which they will take future distributions*, or *income benefit value*, by a predetermined fixed percentage per year, depending upon the insurance company used. Variable annuity insurance contracts will grow the *income benefit value* by capturing an investor's gains and locking them in for future income purposes from daily, quarterly, or annual snapshots of the **contract value** during the accumulation phase prior to the investor taking income for life.

In the distribution phase, variable annuities allow investors to have a predictable stream of income, where the payments are based upon a percentage of the *income benefit value*, per year for a lifetime. Depending upon the particular variable annuity contract, during the distribution phase the investor can get age based, or performance based raises, or both! Typically there are three important concepts in connection with the *income benefit value* during the distribution phase: (1) the guaranteed annual lifetime income *can never go down*, even if the underlying account value or *contract value* declines; (2) the annual payment amount, typically paid out in monthly installments, *can never run out*, as long as the investor lives, or as long as the surviving spouse lives if a surviving spousal rider is added; and (3) the *income benefit value* can continue to grow, even once an investor is taking an income stream in retirement.

The *contract value* is the value of the sum of all the investments inside the variable annuity. If an investor were to transfer or sell the entire contract *after the minimum holding period*, he or she would receive the *contract value* and NOT the income benefit value. It is important for investors to understand this distinction. Many investors, who are still in the accumulation phase, and still saving for retirement, are keeping an inordinate amount of money in cash, money market instruments, or low yielding CDs, because they are fearful their retirement will be compromised if they take on the risk of investing. While the *income benefit value* is not a "walk-away value," or one you can cash out the contract for, it is highly useful for investors in the accumulation phase. The *income benefit value* allows investors approaching retirement to invest with a sense of confidence that regardless of when they turn on the income stream, *the amount from which their distribution amounts will be based* in retirement will grow at a predetermined amount during the accumulation phase, regardless of how the investments and *contract value* perform. At retirement investors can take guaranteed lifetime income distributions from the greater of the *contract value* or the *income benefit value*.

While variable annuities carry greater illiquidity and typically a higher total cost than other investment options, variable annuities can be attractive to investors for more than the traditional death benefit, tax deferred growth in a non-retirement or taxable account, and ability to invest in subaccounts. Variable annuities are also attractive for the guarantee of income for life *without annuitization* during the distribution phase in retirement, regardless of how the investments perform, and the guaranteed growth of the *income benefit value* during the accumulation phase. After suffering a ten-year secular bear market (2000 to 2010), many investors are not willing to take on the full risk of the stock market without any guarantees. The market drawdown was approximately 48% from September 1st 2000 to October 9th 2002, and the market decline of October 9th 2007 to March 9th 2009 was approximately 55% (Carlisle, 2014)! Other significant "intra-year" stock market drawdowns that exceed 10%, that occurred since the two cited above include: -15.99% in 2010, -19.39% in 2011, and -12.35% in 2015 (Short, 2015). Furthermore, low interest rates make it difficult to live off the interest of CDs and other fixed rate investments for one's entire portfolio. Therefore it is not surprising that many income investors are choosing variable annuities for part of a portfolio.

When discussing guarantees relative to an annuity – fixed, immediate, variable or otherwise - you may want to consider the financial strength of the insurance company that issues the annuity contract that you are considering buying. Ultimately, any guarantees are based on the claims-paying ability of the issuing insurance company. Guarantees apply to minimum income from an annuity; they do not guarantee an investment return or the safety of the underlying funds. However, there are variable annuities that allow for an investor to choose a "principal protection" rider, where the investor, after a waiting period, often 10 years, can "walk away" with his or her principal, even if the contract value is less than the purchase price. Additionally, when discussing riders in conjunction with the variable annuity, keep in mind that these are typically purchased at the time that the contract is issued and the investor may incur an additional cost for this option.

III. Practice #3 Don't Forget Stocks

*"The game of speculation is the most uniformly fascinating
game in the world. But it is not a game for the stupid, the
mentally lazy, the man of inferior emotional balance, or
for the get-rich-quick adventurer. They will die poor."*
JESSE LIVERMORE (LIVERMORE & SMITTEN, 2001, P. 1)

Have you ever wished you were Bill Gates and you owned a large percentage of Microsoft? Or maybe you wished you were Steve Jobs and you had started Apple? Maybe you would be set financially if you had only chosen to work for a fast growing company. A share of **stock** is an ownership stake in a publicly traded business, where shareholders can participate in the potential success of a company, through potential share price appreciation, and for companies that pay dividends, a potential increase in the company's quarterly dividend payout to shareholders. On the flip side, they will also need to be comfortable riding out potential drawdowns in the price of the stock as well as reductions or even eliminations of dividends. Dividends are not guaranteed.

Licensed from www.cartoonstock.com

Stock prices tend to rise as the earnings per share of a company increases and the company becomes more successful, and stock prices tend to fall in value as the earnings per share of a company decreases and the company's performance declines. Stock prices tend to look forward into the future and appreciate in price when a catalyst for change is presented that has a high probability of increasing earnings, such as new products, new services, or new management (Edwards, 2015). For example, a company's share price could jump significantly if the company were to bring back the original, beloved founder, and could also rocket higher if a new product is introduced successfully to the market. Some stocks will also pay shareholders a quarterly **dividend** or payout of part of a company's earnings to shareholders.

Individual Stock and Stock Market Valuation

With the ability to grow in price and increase dividends, owning stocks is one of the ways potentially to stay ahead of inflation and to grow your asset base and your income. However, how does an investor know if a stock, or the stock market as a whole, is attractively priced, and it is a good time to buy? First, let's take a look at individual stocks. In order to compare stocks on an "apples to apples" basis, one must NOT compare *stock prices*, but compare *stock valuations*.

For example, Stock A may be priced at $100 per share and earn $10.00 per share, while Stock B may be priced at $50.00 and earn $2.00 per share. Which stock is "cheaper"? While Stock A's share price is higher at $100.00 per share than Stock B's share price at $50.00 a share, in this example Stock A is "cheaper", because its P/E multiple, or price multiple *relative to* earnings, is less than Stock B's P/E multiple. Stock A's price earnings multiple is 10 ($100.00 share price/$10.00 earnings per share = a price earnings multiple of 10). In contrast, Stock B's is higher with a price earnings multiple of 25 ($50.00 share price/ $2.00 earnings per share = a price earnings multiple of 25). Just because a stock's price is lower relative to another's does not necessarily mean it is less expensive!

In addition to P/E multiples, stock analysts and investors can use other valuation metrics to determine if stocks are undervalued, fair valued, or overvalued. Some of the most common valuation metrics used to value companies and compare them to one another are P/E or price to earnings, P/B or price to book value, P/S or price to sales, and P/C or price to cash flow. While P/E is one of the oldest and most common metrics used and discussed in stock valuations, many analysts, investors, and portfolio managers prefer using one or some of the other aforementioned valuation metrics. For example, while the P/E measures, the valuation ratio of a company's current share price compared to its per-share earnings, the P/B Ratio is a ratio used to compare a stock's market value to its book value. It is calculated by dividing the current closing price of the stock by the latest quarter's book value per share. The P/S ratio uses the market capitalization of a company and divides it by the past 12 months' revenues from sales. Finally, the P/C ratio measures the share price relative to the cash flow per share between a firm and its owners and creditors. When analyzing a large conglomerate, investors will typically analyze each part separately and then add up the sum of all the parts, in a method appropriately referred to as a *sum of the parts analysis.*

Different sectors tend to trade at a historical premium valuation or discount valuation to the market, and different stocks tend to trade at a historical premium or historical discount to their peer group or sector. In general, companies that are growing their earnings very rapidly tend to trade at much higher P/E multiples than the market and are called **growth stocks**. In contrast, **value stocks** are companies that are out of favor, growing slowly, and or inconsistently, are priced at a discount to the market, and typically pay out a dividend greater than the market average. Analysts, portfolio managers, and investors who practice **fundamental analysis** focus on valuation, earnings, and tangible changes with management, products, or services at a particular company.

Technical Analysis

Livermore, the famous stock market trader, was correct in his simple maxim: "in a bull market stocks go up – in a bear market they go down," explaining that stocks tend to follow the general direction of the market, going up in bull markets, or upward trending markets, and going down in bear markets, or downward trending markets (Livermore & Smitten, 2001, p.178). 75% of all stocks tend to follow the direction of the stock market as a whole (Investors.com,

2015). The technique of looking at stock market charts or prices and trading volume data to determine patterns or trends about the stock market, or an individual stock, is called **technical analysis** (Hallman & Rosenbloom, 2015, p.110). While technical analysis is as complex and as difficult to perform successfully as fundamental analysis, the focus of technical analysis is to use price and volume charts to buy stocks when they are rising in price and breaking out of a trading range on high volume, and sell stocks that are breaking out on the downside and declining from trading range on high volume (Hallman & Rosenbloom, 2015, p.110).

This technique can be quite effective for determining when to buy or sell an individual stock or the market as a whole. Also, when the 50 day moving average crosses over the 200 day moving average to the upside on high volume, technical analysts take this as a signal that the market is moving into an up-trending or bull market (stockopedia.com, 2015). In contrast, when the 50 day moving average crosses over the 200 day moving average to the downside on high volume, technical analysts take this as a signal that the market is moving into a down-trending or bear market (stockopedia.com, 2015). Watching for the moving average crossover between the 50 and 200 day moving average can help investors determine when the market is changing direction and when to buy or add stocks to a portfolio or sell or lighten up on stocks in a portfolio (stockopedia.com, 2015). The same moving average crossover technique can be applied to individual stocks as well. One can simultaneously utilize the combination of the 5 day moving average, the 10 day moving average, and the 20 day moving average to demonstrate the effectiveness of using the moving average crossover technique to spot a change in an individual stock's direction, whether up or down (Bojinov, 2015).

Is the Market Undervalued or Overvalued?

While investors who follow technical analysis can look at charts to attempt to predict the market direction and whether it is a good time to buy, sell, or hold stocks, how do investors who follow fundamental analysis decide whether the price is right for stocks and it is a good time to buy, sell, or hold? Some investors compare the historical average P/E ratio of 14 to the P/E of today's market. By this metric, with the current S&P P/E ratio of approximately 21.2 as of October 15th 2015, would suggest the stock market is "overvalued" because it is significantly higher than the historical average P/E (www.money. cnn.com/data/markets/sandp/, October, 2015). The median ten-year compounded total return has been consistently higher when stocks were bought with relatively low price earnings multiples, while the median ten-year total return has been consistently lower when stocks were bought with relatively high price earnings multiples (Davis, Allaga-Diaz, Thomas, 2012, p. 12). One could also compare the current market to historical averages for other valuation metrics, like price to book value, price to sales, or price to cash flow.

Another common method to determine where the stock market should be priced is the Fed's Stock Valuation Model (FSVM) utilized by the Federal Reserve Board. The FSVM compares the yield on the ten-year US Treasury Bond to the owner's earnings yield on the stock market, as measured by the S&P 500 benchmark index of US stocks (Samaha, 2014). For example, the current P/E ratio of the S&P 500 stock market index is approximately 21.2 (www.money. cnn.com/data/markets/sandp/, October, 15th 2015) and the owner's earning's yield for the stock market is 4.71% (21.2 P/E for the stock market becomes E/P or 1/21.2 or a 4.71% owners earning's yield for the S&P 500 benchmark index). In comparison, the current yield on the 10-year US Treasury bond is approximately 2.01% (www.bloomberg.com/markets/rates-bonds/government-bonds/us, October 15th 2015). Assuming hypothetically the 10-year US Treasury bond were to remain constant at 2.01%, a P/E of 49.82 for the stock market, or E/P of 1/49.82 (which equals 2.01%), would be reasonable to create an equalization or parity between stocks and bonds. Stocks could appreciate approximately 2.35 fold under this scenario to bring the stock market at parity with the bond market (P/E of 21.2 X 2.35 = P/E of 49.82 or E/P of 1/49.82 or 2.01%). Clearly, all else being equal, as of October 15th 2015, stocks are very cheap relative to bonds when utilizing the FSVM.

Why it is important for an income investor to understand stocks, market timing, valuation metrics, growth and value stocks, and fundamental and technical analysis? Amongst other things - Inflation! Inflation! Inflation! For example, an investor with an investment objective of income, can receive income from dividend paying stocks, yet also address a goal of keeping up with inflation, with the potential for share price appreciation and the potential for rising dividend payments.

III. A. Dividend Paying Stocks

I nvestors face a dilemma: how do I keep up with inflation, invest to potentially grow my capital, and receive income to live off while I wait for capital appreciation? **Dividend paying stocks**, or shares of ownership in publicly traded companies that pay investors quarterly, in the form of dividends, may be worth considering!

A study from *Ned Davis Research* in 2014 sought to demonstrate the performance of dividend paying stocks vs. stocks that do not pay a dividend. The study reported that from 1972 to 2013, while dividend payers averaged 9.3%, and dividend payers that grew their dividend or initiated one averaged 10.1%, the S&P 500 index averaged only 7.6% (Schwartz, 2014).

Clearly it can make sense for investors looking for income to be focusing on dividend paying stocks that are growing their quarterly dividend payout. Typically stocks of companies that are more consistent, and regularly increasing their quarterly earnings, are the same stocks that are consistently raising their quarterly dividend (Moroney, 2013). In addition, since dividends can be eliminated or reduced without notice just like they can be raised or increased without notice, investors should be vigilant to identify stocks that are cutting their dividends or in danger of cutting their dividend. Investors should be particularly cautious about stocks where a company's dividend is unusually high relative to its peer group (Bary, 2015). Often an extraordinarily high dividend is a result of a sharp drop in a company's share price because of a recent adverse earnings report, management change, or other adverse circumstance. Dividend paying stocks are more commonly found in certain market sectors or industries. For example, established, large capitalization stocks are often dividend paying stocks. Value stocks are more mature slower growing businesses, and typically pay out higher dividends than the stock market as a whole, rather than investing 100% of their earnings back into their business. In contrast, it is rarer for growth stocks and small capitalization stocks to pay dividends. Since dividend paying stocks are found more commonly in certain market sectors, it is important for dividend investors to be careful not to concentrate too much of their capital in any one sector. After the credit crises and subprime mortgage market collapse in 2008 investors in banks and financial sector stocks learned the lesson "do not over concentrate in one sector" the hard way!

III. B. Preferred Stocks

A **preferred stock** is a share of ownership in a publicly traded corporation, where investors have the right to be paid dividends before the common shareholders, but are junior to the bondholders in the case of bankruptcy (Hallman & Rosenbloom, 2015, pp. 150-151; Spiegeleer, Schoutens, & Hulle, 2014, pp. 3-4). Preferred stocks are typically issued at $25.00 per share, pay a high rate of interest relative to the dividend payment of the company's common stock, or the coupon payment of the company's bond, and are perpetual, or have long maturities of 30 to 45 years.

Similar to a bond, a preferred stock typically trades close to par value, or the $25.00 issue price, and is typically purchased by investors for the primary goal of income, rather than capital appreciation. Unlike common stocks, which will make sharp moves up or down following an earnings report, preferred stocks will move more with interest rates like long term bonds do. High quality preferred stocks have a high *duration* or interest rate sensitivity, similar to long term high quality bonds, and can drop significantly in price in a rising interest rate environment. In addition, preferred stocks will make sharp moves if the credit rating of the issuer is cut or is likely to be cut, or the viability of the issuer is questionable.

During the credit crises in 2008, Bear Stearns preferred stock issuance was trading at a steep discount to the $25.00 par value, prior to JP Morgan acquiring Bear Stearns and assuming the obligation on all of Bear Stearns's debt and preferred stock. After the acquisition, the Bear Stearns preferred stock went up dramatically, and began trading like JP Morgan preferred stock. A company has to halt the dividend payment on its common stock altogether before it can suspend the dividend payment on the preferred stock. A **cumulative preferred stock** is a preferred stock that is required to pay back all dividends that were suspended prior to reinstating the dividend on the common stock.

Companies in the financial and banking sector issue most of the preferred stocks (Bigda, 2014). Since there is such a concentration of finance and banking companies in the preferred stock universe, it is important for investors to be cognizant of the higher level of volatility and risk associated with investing in one market sector.

While investors may not be able to replicate the preferred stock purchases of Warren Buffet, the long-term return for preferred stocks has been greater than that of corporate bonds, but less than the average long term return common stock holders have achieved.

III. C. Utility Stocks

> *"The stock is for widows and orphans*
> *now. Welcome to middle age, Bill."*
> HENRY HEWITT, MANAGER OF THE
> LIGHT REVOLUTION FUND
> (LA MONICA, 2004)

When Henry Hewitt referred to Microsoft as a stock for widows and orphans, he was making an analogy that Bill Gates's Microsoft, with its slow growth and dividend, was like a stodgy utility stock. Utility stocks have traditionally been popular with income investors for their perceived stability and income.

How Do Investors Percieve Utility Stocks?

Utility stocks have historically been considered relatively safe by investors because they are issued by companies that supply essential basic necessary services like water, electricity, and telecommunications, typically have a geographic monopoly, and there are high cost barriers for competitors to enter the market. An additional characteristic of utility stocks is that they tend to have a very low correlation to the stock market as a whole (Carnevale, 2015). Modern Portfolio Theory statistics confirm the low correlation of utility stocks to the S&P 500 benchmark stock index. Utilities grow slowly with the population and general demand for basic services such as electricity, water, and heating. Therefore they tend to fluctuate more like investment grade bonds, with sensitivity to interest rates and inflation, than act like stocks, which move more with the ups and downs of the economic cycle.

How to mitigate some risk in Utility Stock Investing

One way investors can manage risk when investing in utility stocks is to look at the payout ratio. The **payout ratio** is the amount paid out in dividends annually, divided by the utility's annual earnings. One theory that some investors subscribe to is that as, a good rule of thumb, investors should look for payout ratios of 60% or lower (Smith, 2013). This provides the utility with a nice margin to continue to raise the dividend, even in inevitable periods of slow growth or no growth. Investors can also mitigate risk by diversifying among utility types within the sector, and diversifying geographically, both domestically and internationally.

III. D. Real Estate Investment Trusts

Having made a fortune in real estate, Donald Trump is known for being a little overzealous in his advocacy for real estate investing. The real estate bubble, credit crises, and subprime mortgage crises in 2008 led to many real estate foreclosures and losses. The credit crises had an adverse effect on REITs, and many had to reduce their dividend payments (Johnson, 2010, p. 62). In the United States, in 2010, one in seven homeowners was either in foreclosure or over 30 days late on their home payment (Adler, 2010). While the most recent credit crises (2007 to 2009) and its' aftermath was not kind to residential real estate investors and REIT investors alike, historically from 1999 through 2014, REITs averaged 12.29%, while the S&P 500 stock market benchmark index averaged 4.24% (www.reit.com, 2015). In the ten years ending in 2014, REITS outperformed inflation and nearly matched stocks, with a 7.5% average return for REITs vs. a 7.67% return for stocks (www.reit.com, 2015).

What is a REIT?

A real estate investment trust or a **REIT** is a non-profit company, public or private, set up for the purpose of investing in real estate, that must invest most of its assets in real estate, and must pay out a minimum of 90% of its income annually to investors in the trust (Younus, 2015, pp. 9-15). While investors must pay taxes on the dividend income from REITs, REITs do not have any federal taxes, in exchange for meeting the requirements above.

Why consider REITs?

Since many of us do not have the means to go out and buy an apartment building with our spare cash, the REIT structure allows income investors to pool their money together to purchase shares in a real estate trust. Many investors avoid direct real estate investing because they do not want the headaches of repairs and tenants. In addition, the time and expertise in selecting and improving properties can be another deterrent to investing directly in real estate. Even if an investor has the funds to buy one property, rarely can he or she have the ability to diversify across a portfolio of real estate properties by directly investing in real estate.

REITs can address many of the problems associated with direct real estate investing by providing the benefit of diversification and professional management. Similar to Utilities, REITs tend to be non-correlated to stocks and move up and down in value, somewhat unrelated to the movements of the S&P 500 (Ferri, 2014; Younus, 2015, pp. 3, 22; Malkiel, 2015, p. 314).

What are the risks of REIT investing?

While the benefits of diversification, professional management, and a low correlation to the stock market are enticing to investors, what are the risks associated with REIT investing? One obvious risk is the risk of real estate in general. There was a time when Donald Trump himself was so devastated by a sharp decline in his leveraged real estate assets that he said he actually had a *negative* net worth (Hathaway, 2015). Real Estate is one sector of the economy, and while investors can diversify among different types of REITs, and different geographies, real estate is cyclical, and much of the sector can be out of favor at once. Therefore most financial planners and investment advisors, all else being equal, would recommend that individual investors limit real estate investment trusts to only a certain percentage of an investment portfolio.

Another risk is leverage (Younus, 2015, p.51). While leverage can enhance returns in times of moderate inflation of asset prices, leverage can eliminate equity ownership altogether in times of deflation, credit crises, and financial collapse. In the credit crises of 2008 and early 2009, many investors were not certain that REITs could obtain financing, and the viability of the REIT sector was in question (Johnson, 2010, pp. 58, 62).

Finally, a sharp rise in interest rates can cause the cost of financing to go up and the prices of real estate to go down. In addition, a sharp rise in interest rates can make the yields on REITs less competitive compared to bond yields and cause a selloff, driving REIT prices lower, until their yields are competitive with current bond yields.

While few income investors will have the means or desire to be a real estate mogul like Donald Trump, REITs can provide a potential opportunity for income and capital appreciation, low correlation to stocks, professional management, and diversification.

III. E. Master Limited Partnerships

nother niche area that income investors have zeroed in on is master limited partnerships. Master limited partnerships are limited partnerships that are publicly traded on a securities exchange just like shares of stock. Predominantly organized for companies engaged in the storage and distribution of oil, gas, and natural resources, **master limited partnerships** allow investors to purchase units of ownership that pay high dividends (Mullaney, 2015).

Furthermore, a majority of the dividends of MLPs are considered a *return of principal*, and therefore do not trigger a high current tax bill for investors (Mullaney, 2015). The dividends of MLPs lower the *cost basis* of the investment, causing a majority of the dividend taxes to be deferred until the security is sold, and then treated as long-term capital gains, which traditionally have been taxed at a more favorable lower rate than dividends (Mullaney, 2015). While the partnership structure of master limited partnerships results in a more favorable tax treatment, one of the hassles investors must consider for this tax deferred high income is receiving a K-1 – versus the traditional 1099 - tax form each year (Mullaney, 2015).

Risks Associated with Master Limited Partnerships

While high income and tax advantages are enticing for income investors, there are some risks that need to be considered prior to making an oversized commitment to MLPs. Since the majority of MLPs focus their business on the storage and distribution of oil and gas, MLP investing is highly sector specific. Therefore it is wise for income investors as a general rule to invest a small percentage of their investment portfolio in MLPs. During the credit crises in 2008 and early 2009, MLPs declined in sympathy to the price of oil declining, and MLPs also dropped because the access to credit and capital became questionable (Lavine, 2013). Holders of MLPs also must consider having limited control and limited voting rights relative to matters affecting the partnership. Additionally, while tax treatment is typically favorable, there could be a risk if a conflict of interest exists between the common unit holders and the general partner, including those arising from incentive distribution payments.

III. F. Writing Covered Calls against Dividend Paying Stocks

Soothsayer: "Beware the ides of March."
Caesar: "What man is that?"
Brutus: "A soothsayer, bids you beware the ides of March."
SHAKESPEARE: *JULIUS CAESAR ACT 1, SCENE 2, 15–19*

Just as Caesar was told by the psychic to be careful of the ides of March, or March 15, which was the day Caesar was assassinated and he *expired*, option buyers and sellers, must be cognizant of option expiration, which is the 3rd Friday of every month! So now that we know what options have to do with Shakespeare, what do options have to do with income investing?

What is a *call option*? A **call option** gives an investor the right to buy a stock at a specified **strike price**, over a specified period of time prior to the option's expiration date, in exchange for an option premium, or option cost paid by the speculator (McInish & Upson, 2015, pp. 41, 45). The covered call is a strategy in which an investor writes or sells a call option contract while at the same time owning an equivalent number of shares of the underlying stock. A covered call writer or seller foregoes participation in any increase in the stock price above the call exercise price and continues to bear the downside risk of stock ownership if the stock price decreases more than the premium received. Keep in mind that if the stock price falls, the investor is still a stock owner, and is subject to the full loss of his or her stock investment, reduced only by the credit from the sale of the Call. Covered Call Selling is not a protective strategy. Also, it is important to keep in mind that when writing an option on a stock with a low cost basis, there are tax consequences to consider upon assignment. When participating in a covered call strategy, the investor is also at risk of having to sell the underlying stock if the stock's price rises above the sold option's strike price. Remember, in exchange for receiving the premium of having sold the call, the investor is obligated to sell the underlying stock via assignment if the option is exercised.

For example, a publicly traded fast food chain is supposed to come out with a new smoothie flavor, Blue-Moon-Blueberry, in June, six months away. While the current price of the fast food chain's stock, is priced at $75 per share, Zachary (an investor who does not wish to purchase the shares outright but would rather potentially profit from short term movements) is confident the company's stock price will soar well past $80 before the debut of the new

Blue-Moon-Berry smoothie, therefore Zachary buys one June call options contract (representing 100 shares) with an $80 strike price for $2.00 per option, for a total premium paid of $200.00. Not including the cost of commissions, Zachary would lose money if the stock traded below $82.00 through option expiration (the strike price of $80.00 + the premium of $2.00 =$82.00 of cost to Zachary). Likewise, if you factor out commissions, Zachary would break even if he were to exercise his option contract at $82.00. Finally, factoring out commissions, Zachary would begin to realize a profit, if he were to exercise his option contract, when the price of the stock is above $82.00 prior to expiration.

An investor such as Zachary would employ this strategy because he is "bullish" in the near term for this stock. He sees the potential for the appreciation of the option's price during the term of the option and then – if things go as Zachary believes it will go – he will be able to sell the call option at a profit sometime prior to expiration. On the other hand, if gains fail to materialize and the likelihood of a pre-expiration rally seems unlikely, if Zachary does not sell the call option and holds it through expiration, the maximum he will lose is the premium paid. It is important to note that the stock and option prices shown are hypothetical and are for illustrative purposes only. There is no guarantee that these prices can or will be duplicated. Commission, dividends, margin, taxes and other transaction charges have not been included. However, they will affect the outcome of the option transaction and should be considered. *Transaction costs are significant and should be considered.* Additionally, because of the importance of tax considerations to all options transactions, investors considering options should consult with their tax advisor to evaluate how taxes can affect the outcome of contemplated options transactions.

At the same time, there is another investor who already owns 100 shares of the fast food chain's stock, believes that the stock's price could appreciate past $80 before June, and wants to generate additional income without adding too much additional risk. In this case, the investor "writes" or sells a call option expiring in June for $2.00. While this investor does keep the premium paid to him when he sold the call, this investor does "forfeit" much of the stock's profit potential given the fact that – should the stock's price appreciate past the strike price – it is increasingly likely that it will be "called away" (the buyer of the option takes possession of the stock at the strike price). In terms of other risks, the maximum loss can be substantial. If the underlying stock price goes to $0.00, the investor will lose the entire value of the stock. However, it will be offset by the premium paid. On the upside, the maximum gains are also limited as the net potential profit to an investor would be the premium received, plus the stock appreciation to the strike price (McInish & Upson, 2015, pp. 41,45,46). This action of selling call options, or *writing* call options against shares of stock an investor already owns, is called **writing a covered call** (McInish & Upson, 2015, pp. 41, 45,46).

In contrast, **writing an uncovered call** is when an option seller does not own shares in the underlying stock yet writes or sells a call. Like covered call writing, the investor keeps the premium received however, uncovered call writing is among the riskiest option strategies, because it exposes the option seller to unlimited market risk. Theoretically, there is no limit on how high a stock price can go, and since the option seller does not own any shares, he or she will have to buy them at the prevailing market price, should the call option be exercised prior to expiration (Hallman & Rosenbloom, 2015, pp. 135-136).

If an investor had to pay $50,000.00 for their son's Harvard MBA tuition, and received $2.00 for each share of stock he sold a covered call option against, and each option contract represented 100 shares, how many contracts would he have to sell? Not considering commission or any transactional fees, the answer is 250. The math is as follows: $2.00 premium x 100 shares = $200.00 per contract; $50,000.00 tuition/$200.00 per contract = 250 contracts. The investor will need to own 25,000 shares (250 contracts x 100 shares per contract = 25,000 shares) of the stock in order to write 250 contracts of *covered calls* against his holdings of the stock.

One powerful strategy employed by some income investors is to buy dividend-paying stocks with a history of increasing their dividends and write covered call options against them to supplement the income. While this does limit an investor's upside to some extent, since the stock can get *called away* at the *strike price* at which the option is sold or written, the additional income can be significant.

IMPORTANT:

Options involve risk and are not suitable for all investors. Before opening an option position, a person must receive a copy of "Characteristics and Risks of Standardized Options". This document is available from The Chicago Board of Options Exchange at www.cboe.com

IV. Practice #4 Understand Investment Structure

"Wide diversification is only required when investors
do not understand what they are doing."

WARREN BUFFETT

We have covered how income investors utilize bonds, annuities, and stocks for income. While annuities qualify as an "investment vehicle", what are the different investment vehicles that income investors may want to consider using to create a diversified portfolio? Should income investors use ETFs, closed-end funds, mutual funds, individual securities, or private asset managers? Maybe income investors should utilize a combination of some of them or all of them? The answer(s) depends upon an investor's goals, risk profile, level of sophistication, tax status, and the level of involvement in day- to-day decisions an investor wants.

IV. A. ETFs

An **ETF** is an exchange-traded fund, where investors pool their money to help achieve diversification and full exposure to a particular passive or unmanaged market index, market sector, or asset class of stocks, bonds, commodities, or other securities. Why do some investors select the ETF structure for all or part of their investment portfolio?

Advantages of ETFs

ETFs offer investors several advantages over other investment vehicles. With the average ETF charging approximately .44% for an internal management fee, many individual and institutional investors are drawn to the low internal management fees of the ETF structure (guides.wsj.com, 2015). Traders are attracted to the intra-day liquidity feature of ETFs. While ETFs can be bought and sold throughout the day, mutual funds are bought and sold once a day. Another attractive feature of ETFs for some investors is their level of tax efficiency.

While most index funds tend to be rather tax efficient, because generally they are not actively managed and have relatively little turnover, or buying and selling that creates capital gains taxes, ETFs have the same tax advantages. While many mutual funds typically liquidate securities to meet the cash demands of investors selling shares, ETFs do not have to sell any securities to meet redemption requests (Patton, 2015). ETFs will pay out the demands of institutions with in-kind distributions of the stocks that comprise the portfolio, and therefore do not have to sell any securities to meet investor distribution requests, like many mutual funds typically do (Patton, 2015). ETFs also utilize in-kind distribution of individual securities to help avoid taxes on more highly appreciated securities. Some mutual funds also utilize in-kind distributions (Farmer & Van Horn, 2014).

While investors can choose their top 5, 10, or 20 stocks to create diversification, ETFs offer investors diversification and exposure to specific markets and sectors of bonds and stocks. Investors who want exposure to a specific country, sector of the economy, or commodity often consider utilizing ETFs. Self-directed traders and aggressive investors may sometimes take advantage of sector ETFs that are leveraged two and three times to enhance their return. As mentioned earlier, the use of leverage can be extremely risky, when one's investment thesis, or bet, does not work out as planned or anticipated. In addition, self-directed traders will use short ETFs to short market sectors, and potentially profit from price declines in market sectors or indices. ETFs that short the major market indices and options on ETFs that short the market indices can also be used to hedge an investment portfolio, or help provide some downside protection from market declines.

Disadvantages of ETFs

While ETFs have many attractive features, they do have some disadvantages – for example, while they may help diversify a portfolio, diversification cannot guarantee a profit in declining markets. When the market or a particular sector is appreciating or trending upward, ETFs that track the market or a particular sector tend to perform well for a very competitive cost. However, in market corrections and downtrends, ETFs will decline in tandem with the market, with no risk management or strategy. Basically ETFs may rise and fall with the market or sector they track like a jellyfish rises and falls with the waves in the ocean, with little or no control of its destiny. Simply put - exchange traded funds are subject to risks similar to those of stocks, bonds, or commodities, depending upon the index or sector they track. Investment returns may fluctuate and are subject to market volatility, so that an investor's shares, when redeemed or sold, may be worth more or less than their original cost.

Actively managed portfolios or investment products are monitored proactively and managed in a way intended to optimize returns and reduce risk. The decade ending in 2010, known as "the lost decade," was a poor one for the major stock market averages, leaving many ETF equity index investors, with little or no return after a ten-year period. Ironically, investors who purchased index funds and ETFs that tracked the major market averages saved on expenses, but still lost on performance. Many actively managed strategies made significant cumulative gains, over the *lost decade*, by having flexibility to go in and out of stocks and bonds, or invest in different types of stock and bonds, and make changes to capitalize on current market conditions, or mitigate risk. While there are ETFs that are actively managed, they are atypical, representing a small percentage of all ETFs. ETFs that track the major stock market averages have done well since the market low in March of 2009. The market drawdown was approximately 48% from September 1st 2000 to October 9th 2002, and the market decline of October 9th 2007 to March 9th 2009 was approximately 55% (Carlisle, 2014)! Other significant "intra-year" stock market drawdowns, that exceed 10%, that occurred since the two cited above include: -15.99% in 2010, -19.39% in 2011, and -12.35% in 2015 (Short, 2015).

During the "flash crash" in the spring of 2010, the Dow Jones Industrial Average dropped nearly 1000 points in one day (Goldfarb, 2010). By allowing for *intra-day trading and pricing*, ETFs gave investors up to the minute pricing, providing them a front row seat to the volatility. Sometimes the common investor behavior of selling at low points and buying at high points is exacerbated by intra-day trading and watching the market play-by-play. In contrast, mutual funds calculate their *net asset value*, or the cumulative value of all the assets within the fund, at the end of the day. By allowing investors to see one price at the end of the day, mutual funds can help to prevent over-trading by investors.

ETFs have the distinct advantages of low cost, tax-efficiency, and targeted investment exposure. In addition, *short* ETFs have the potential to profit from downward trending markets, or hedge a portfolio. However, the lack of active management to optimize risk and return, a high degree of intra-day volatility, and potential commission costs to buy and sell ETFs can present challenges for ETF investors.

IV. B. Closed-End Funds

"Most people get interested in stocks when everyone else is. The time to get interested is when no one else is. You can't buy what is popular and do well."

WARREN BUFFETT (SCHLESINGER, 2010)

What if an investor liked the features of an ETF, but preferred active management over a passive index? A **closed-end fund** is a close cousin of an ETF, in the sense that it is a diversified fund traded intra-day, often representing a diversified portfolio of a certain sector or type of stock or bond. A *closed-end fund* is *actively managed* (Brewer, 2015). Closed-end funds are investment companies that are registered with the U.S. Securities and Exchange Commission. Generally created by large asset management firms, closed-end funds are managed pools of investments that trade on a stock exchange. Unlike an open-end fund which continually issues new shares to investors who buy shares in the fund (and continually redeems shares from investors), a closed-end fund generally offers only a fixed number of shares.

Advantages of Closed-End Funds

The net asset value (NAV) of a closed-end fund is the market value of the underlying investments (i.e., stocks and bonds) in the fund's portfolio, minus liabilities, divided by the total number of fund shares outstanding. This definition is the same for closed-end and open-end funds. However, the closed-end fund also has a market price; the value at which it trades on an exchange. This price can be more or less than its NAV. Therefore, the NAV of a closed-end fund may not be the price you pay for a share of the fund. In contrast, at the end of the day mutual funds are priced at closing net asset value, or NAV, or the sum or cumulative price of all of the securities owned by the funds.

While the ability to purchase closed-end funds at a discount to NAV is a highly attractive feature, investors must be cognizant that discounts can persist for long periods of time and some funds have a history of trading at a discount. Before purchasing a fund at a discount it is important to research if the fund has historically traded at a discount, and if so, what has been the average discount. For income investors, purchasing closed-end funds at a discount allows investors to receive yields that are higher than those afforded in the market.

Furthermore, yields can be enhanced further with leveraged closed-end funds. As always, leverage is a double- edged sword, while leverage enhances yields, it creates additional risk by magnifying losses. Another attractive feature of a closed-end fund is the fact that the manager has a finite or static quantity of investor capital to manage. Closed-end funds will raise capital through an initial public offering. Afterwards, the price relative to the fund's NAV is determined by a number of factors including the fund's investment strategy and the underlying asset class in which it invests, its current distribution rate and total return potential, and supply vs. demand for the shares, to name a few. As a result, closed-end funds are intended to be long-term investments and should not be used as short-term trading vehicles.

Challenges of Closed-End Funds

While closed-end funds have many advantages and attractive features, challenges remain. As mentioned earlier, while leverage can magnify yields, leverage can be a double-edged sword, magnifying losses. While investors can benefit from buying closed-end funds at a discount, investors also need to be cautious about purchasing closed-end funds at a *premium*. Closed-end funds can trade or price at a premium, or higher amount than the aggregate value of their internal holdings, due to market demand. While premiums can persist for long periods of time, without highly advantageous market conditions rarely will the net asset value increase to meet the level of a closed-end fund priced at a significant premium.

Closed-End Funds are actively managed and can employ a number of investment strategies in pursuit of the fund's objectives. Some strategies may increase the overall risk of the fund and there is no assurance that any investment strategy will be successful or that the fund will achieve its intended objective. Closed-end funds are subject to different risks, volatility, fees and expenses. Many closed-end funds can leverage their assets to enhance yields. Leverage is a speculative technique that exposes a portfolio to increased risk of loss, may cause fluctuations in the market value of the fund's portfolio which could have a disproportionately large effect on the fund's NAV or cause the NAV of the fund generally to decline faster than it would otherwise. The use of leverage and other risk factors are more fully described in each closed-end fund's prospectus under the heading "Risks."

IV. C. Mutual Funds

"Because mutual funds can offer built-in diversification and professional management, they offer certain advantages over purchasing individual stocks and bonds. But, like investing in any security, investing in a mutual fund involves certain risks, including the possibility that you may lose money."(FINRA.ORG 2014)

Diversification and Professional Management

A mutual fund, or open-end fund, is an investment vehicle, in which investors pool their money together to purchase shares of an *actively, professionally managed* and *diversified* portfolio of stocks, bonds, and/or other securities. Two of the primary functions of the mutual fund structure are diversification and active professional management. While James Cramer of CNBC insists that investors should pick stocks on their own (with his advice of course), many investors lack the time, knowledge, or desire to manage their own portfolio of stocks or bonds. Investors need

60 stocks in a portfolio to achieve the level of diversification that substantially eliminates unsystematic risk, or risk that is unique to a particular stock (Malkiel, 2015, pp. 211-212).

Licensed from www.cartoonstock.com

More Advantages of Mutual Funds

From Dynamic Investing to Sector Specific Exposure. Similar to ETFs, mutual funds can give investors exposure to specific countries, sectors, or types of securities. However, mutual funds allow for active management. Mutual funds may have a broader investment philosophy. For example, a mutual fund may be able to purchase stocks and bonds, or high yield as well as investment grade bonds.

By allowing for *dynamic* investing with a flexible investment philosophy, where the fund manager can change the types of securities depending upon market conditions, mutual funds have the potential to mitigate risk and take advantage of *special situations*, or temporary dislocations in specific asset classes that could present an investment opportunity. During the credit crises of 2008 and early 2009, the spread between high yield corporate debt and treasuries soared to over 21% (Aneiro, 2014). This was an anomaly that a bond mutual fund manager with a broad investment thesis could have capitalized upon, by purchasing high yield debt at a discount, and opening the potential for profit when the spread between high yield bonds and treasuries narrowed significantly. The current spread between high yield bonds and treasuries is approximately 4.3% as of October 15th 2015.

Monthly Income. Furthermore, bonds are usually a significant percentage of an overall portfolio for income investors. However bonds typically pay interest in six-month intervals, making it difficult to choose the bonds appropriate for a particular investor's situation but also choose suitable bonds that pay at different times to create a steady monthly income stream. In contrast, a mutual fund might pay dividends on a *monthly basis*, which could help address an investor's need for monthly income.

NAV Pricing. An additional feature of open-end mutual funds is that they are bought and sold at *closing net asset value*. The caveat to keep in mind is that some share classes of mutual funds can have "up front" or "back end" charges associated with buying and selling. The collective value of all of the individual holdings inside the mutual fund at the end of each day is the **closing net asset value.** Since mutual funds price at the closing net asset value, this can be beneficial in allowing investors to take a longer term outlook and not to get caught up too much in short term trading as the investors would not have to watch extreme price movements in the course of a day.

Liquidity, commissions, and fee-based wrap accounts. While mutual fund investors typically cannot purchase and sell their funds intra-day, besides a handful of fund families including Rydex and Profunds, they do have daily liquidity. While most mutual funds are designed for the purpose of long-term investing, the daily liquidity feature can be attractive for both cash disbursement needs and re-balancing a portfolio.

As your objectives change, you can switch among the mutual funds in the same mutual fund family without incurring an additional sales charge (as long as the fund doesn't charge fees for moving money from one fund to another). Staying within the same mutual fund family may be preferable, because switching from one mutual fund family to another may involve additional costs or fees.

On the other hand, there may be legitimate reasons to switch or exchange to a mutual fund in another mutual fund family, or another type of investment product, when the original mutual fund family does not offer the type of investment product you are interested in. If you do choose to switch to a mutual fund in a different mutual fund family or to another type of investment, and your account is based on commission (as opposed to being a "fee-based" or wrap account where an investor is charged an annual asset based fee, and typically assessed ¼ of the annual fee each quarter based upon the value of the account), you will most likely incur a sales charge on the new investment. In addition to the new sales charge, you may be subject to either a front-end sales charge or a back-end sales charge dependent on the type of mutual fund. A Class A mutual fund share has a front-end load that is paid at the time the fund is purchased. While the charge varies from one fund company to another, typically the charge is about 5%. This amount is subtracted from the total you're investing in the fund. A Class B share carries a back-end sales charge or "contingent deferred sales charge" based on a specified redemption period (typically 7 years), that you are required to pay on any of your shares that you sell during that period. Finally, a Class C share may carry a "level load" (a fee charged for every year the fund is held) or may have a back-end load similar to Class B shares, which typically is 1% and is only charged if the shares sold are held less than one year. It is important to note that Class C shares do not convert to another share class. In those instances when a mutual fund switch to a different mutual fund or to another investment product results in a new commission charged, you will receive a mutual fund switch letter. This letter discloses general information regarding your switch, including the potential availability of an exchange within your existing open-end mutual fund family, as well as the possibility of additional costs and expenses.

You should also be aware that there may be tax consequences related to your sale, redemption or exchange of mutual fund shares. If you have questions about the possible tax consequences of a sale, redemption or exchange of your mutual fund shares, you should consult your tax advisor prior to making any such investment decision.

It is also important for you to consider how your overall investment may be impacted by a mutual fund switch, depending on the type of fund you own.

Low Minimums. Finally, another one of the advantages of mutual funds is that they can be purchased with a low minimum threshold for investment. However, keep in mind that other securities such as ETFs or stocks also share this benefit of allowing for the purchase in small dollar amounts. This allows investors the ability to diversify among several funds and allows investors to invest a small amount each month and **dollar cost average** into mutual funds. While not assuring a profit or protecting against loss, by dollar cost averaging, or buying shares of a fund at regular intervals, this allows investors to purchase at different price points and market conditions.

Disadvantages of Mutual Funds

While diversification, active professional management, ability to invest dynamically with a broader investment philosophy, ability to pay monthly income, typically utilizing NAV pricing, high liquidity, and a low minimum required investment are some of the attractive features of mutual funds, they do have some drawbacks.

Taxation of Mutual Funds. In a brokerage account, or an account that is subject to taxation, and not a tax deferred retirement account, mutual funds can create challenges for managing taxes. Unlike when purchasing an individual security, where an individual investor who purchases a stock or bond receives his own personal cost basis for tax purposes, in a mutual fund an investor must pay taxes on all capital gains tax distributions of the fund, regardless of whether the investor owned the fund during the period of gain. While it doesn't happen often, and investors can check capital gains exposure of mutual funds prior to purchase, investors in mutual funds can end up paying taxes on gains they did not personally receive. It is important to note that tax deferred accounts such as IRA accounts and 401(k) accounts are not subject to taxation unless distributions are made, and in that case the investor pays taxes based upon the amount he or she decided to distribute, irrespective of any capital gains realized by the mutual funds in the IRA or 401(k). However it is important for investors investing outside of a qualified retirement plan, IRA, or 401(k) to be cognizant of any capital gains exposure of a fund prior to purchase.

Typically funds will make a capital gains distribution once a year. One strategy that an investor may employ is to purchase funds after a capital gains distribution has already been made, in order to prevent the situation of an investor paying taxes on gains he or she did not individually receive. Furthermore, low turnover funds tend to buy and sell less, and therefore have the potential to create less of a tax bill. While it is important to be tax aware, investors need to be careful to make proper investments based upon their unique risk profile and return goals, without solely focusing on the tax ramifications.

Transparency. Another challenge mutual fund investor's face is transparency. While the statement of additional information is released monthly or semi-annually and contains all of a mutual fund's holdings, it is not updated daily, and typically cannot be pulled up on a daily basis for investors to know what they own. Investors can also cope with the transparency issue of mutual funds by looking up the top ten holdings, or obtaining a fact sheet from a mutual fund company. One of the problems mutual fund investors have faced is that when markets are declining, investors cannot see the companies they own, and therefore often cash out during downturns, hurting their long-term performance. This behavior can be mitigated by investors researching the holdings of their funds and the investment thesis or strategy employed by the mutual fund manager or management, or using an investment advisor or financial consultant to understand the holdings and strategy behind a fund.

Size. The growing size of an open-end fund or mutual fund can also pose a problem, particularly in the small capitalization stock arena. For example, let's imagine that a successful small capitalization stock mutual fund attracts many new investors. However, when a small cap mutual fund grows too large, it can no longer purchase small companies because the dollar amount wouldn't make a significant impact on the fund. This phenomenon causes many great small cap funds to style drift and re-brand, or drift to a mid-cap or a large cap focus.

Managing Cash Flows. Another drawback of the open-end structure is the need for a mutual fund portfolio manager to manage cash flows. Because open-end funds are issuing more shares to new investors, and issuing cash to investors making disbursements, mutual fund managers sometimes will be forced to sell securities at times that may be less than "ideal", for the sole purpose of meeting investor redemptions. In addition, sometimes a large influx of cash comes in at once diluting the existing holdings of the fund until the mutual fund manager is able to invest it.

While the issues of taxation, transparency, size, and managing cash flows are all drawbacks of investing in mutual funds, for many investors these issues are easily outweighed by the benefits of mutual funds, including the active dynamic professional investment management, diversification, low minimums, and potential for generating consistent monthly income.

IV. D. Individual Securities

W hy would an investor consider foregoing mutual funds, ETFs, closed-end funds, and private asset managers and other investment vehicles and pick individual stocks and bonds on their own? Often an investment managed by someone else, whether actively or passively managed, is not well understood or appreciated. Many investors like to know what they own. They want to see, touch, and feel their investment portfolio. By selecting the stocks, bonds, and other securities and building the portfolio from scratch, investors can have confidence, knowledge, and conviction about each individual holding. Understanding one's investments can be helpful as investors may be able to more easily hold on during difficult markets, with the knowledge that they hold investments that can weather the storm.

Tax Implications

As mentioned earlier, investments held outside of an IRA, 401(k), or other qualified tax deferred retirement plan, are subject to taxes when sold at a profit. By utilizing individual securities, investors can control their own personal cost basis on each individual holding and have tax control to buy and sell securities and balance out gains and losses when appropriate for tax considerations. As of tax year 2014, investors may take up to $3,000.00 per year in excess losses which are greater than the amount of gains, in an account subject to taxation, or a regular account, as an income tax deduction. Additionally, as of tax year 2014, if losses exceed the $3,000.00 threshold in any given year, investors may carry forward the losses to be used against further gains.

Bond or CD Ladder

Often investors will purchase bonds or CDs for income and to help smooth out the performance of their portfolio. While the monthly income and active management of mutual funds has an allure for some investors, many investors want to know exactly what they own and eliminate management costs. For example, an investor can buy new issue bonds, where the bonds are issued at $1,000.00 per bond with no mark up or commission. The investment firm is paid an underwriting fee by the corporate or municipal issuer; therefore the individual investor is not charged a fee or commission. Bonds can also be found in the secondary market that may be more attractive, *even after a commission is charged!*

One technique is to create a **bond ladder**, where bonds are purchased that mature at regular intervals, with shorter term maturities purchased to protect against interest rate risk, and longer term maturities purchased to protect against reinvestment risk. This ladder may go out 5, 10, 15 years or longer. Each time a bond comes due, the investor buys a new bond at the long end of the ladder. For example, an investor has invested in bonds maturing in 2,4,6,8 and 10 years. Two years from the initial purchase when the 2 year bond matures and the proceeds are in the investor's account, the investor would purchase a bond with a 10 year maturity in order to maintain the ladder. While bond laddering doesn't guarantee a profit or protect against loss in a declining market, the goal of purchasing a ladder of bonds in varying maturities is to provide returns higher than if only short-term maturities were purchased but with less risk than a portfolio comprised solely of long-term maturities.

Stock Portfolio

While income investors can utilize both fundamental and technical analysis to choose individual dividend paying stocks, this exercise can require a lot of time and knowledge. The risk of the market as a whole is *systemic risk*. The risk of one individual company is *un-systemic risk*. While investors can be rewarded handsomely by purchasing a few individual dividend-paying stocks, they can also be punished severely for purchasing the wrong dividend paying stocks. Based upon a variety of individual factors, financial advisors will typically recommend that investors hold no more than a certain percentage of their net worth in any one stock, especially those investors that are within 5 to 10 years of retirement, or currently in retirement.

When selecting individual stocks there is a great deal of un-systemic risk, unique to the individual company. While there are great success stories - such as a company highlighted on the news for growth from its issuance to over $100 a share - there are other companies on the other end of the spectrum, highlighted for their meteoric rise and subsequent decline. One important nuance to note is the fact that a company can raise, drop or completely eliminate a dividend. For example, let's imagine that a natural disaster occurred and an established, dividend paying company's major facilities were destroyed by this natural disaster. The company may choose to suspend its dividend to repair facilities and deal with any subsequent aftereffects of the crisis. While investors can build a diversified portfolio of dividend-paying stocks, which would eliminate or diversify away un-systemic risk, it would take tremendous time, knowledge, and effort.

Stop Loss vs. Stop Limit Order

One strategy that can further mitigate risk when purchasing individual stocks, one at a time, is using a stop loss. A sell **stop loss order**, or a sell stop, is when an investor purchases a stock and then subsequently places a sell order at a lower price that – when the specified stop price is met - the stop order becomes a market order and executes at the next available price. Depending on market conditions, this may mean that the execution price may be several points away from the stop price (higher or lower). This is a strategy intended to provide an investor with a method to objectively exit a stock position by defining an exit point in advance of a stock's potential decline. Sometimes a stock will open up at a much lower price than the previous day's trading session, one even lower than an investor would want to sell it at. Therefore investors will sometimes use a **stop limit order**, which is a type of order that combines the features of a stop order with those of a limit order. A stop-limit order will be executed at a specified price (or better) after a given stop price has been reached. Once the stop price is reached by the market, the stop-limit order becomes a limit order to buy (or sell) at the limit price or better.

While some investors may be attracted to the transparency, tax control, and low cost of owning individual securities outright, the great deal of time and knowledge required to manage a portfolio of individual securities, outweighs the excitement of selecting individual securities for many investors.

IV. E. Private Asset Managers

"I mean it's the most objective industry in the world. If your numbers stink, you're out. If your numbers are good, you get more money. It's the most Darwinian, it's beautiful, it's brutal, it works."
JIM CRAMER (PBS, FRONTLINE, 1995-2010)

An account managed by a **private asset manager**, sometimes referred to as a separately managed account or managed account, is a private portfolio of stocks, bonds, or securities that is diversified, and professionally and actively managed. Some would say that a private asset manager seeks to combine the "best of both worlds", having the benefit of diversification and active professional management, yet having a private portfolio of individual securities, with a private cost basis and transparency like a portfolio of individual securities an investor would select on his or her own.

When considering a privately managed account as such, one must keep in mind their personal situation and what is suitable. This is a type of advisory account and advisory accounts are not designed for either excessively traded or inactive accounts, meaning that it may not be suitable for all investors. When signing up for this type of account, be sure to read the advisory disclosure documents for a full description of services, fees and expenses.

Private Asset Manager vs. Other Investment Vehicles

Higher Minimum Investment. Originally, private asset managers only managed money for institutions and high net worth investors with minimum account sizes of $1,000,000.00 or more. Most nationally recognized investment firms now grant access to these private asset managers for $100,000.00 minimums per asset manager. While the minimum is reduced, it is not eliminated. Some investors do not have enough capital to diversify properly across several separately managed accounts and also meet the minimum requirement of each private asset manager.

A Limited Menu of Private Asset Managers. There may only be 50 to 100 private asset managers to choose from, and strategies offered may not be as broad, flexible, or diverse as compared to other investment options. Furthermore if the particular private asset manager desired is available, he or she may not be available at every national investment firm, as they are bound by individual arrangements.

Income Objective. The theme of a limited menu is clear when it comes to bond, REIT, utility, balanced (stocks and bonds), high yield bond, preferred stock, and other income strategies. While some nationally recognized investment firms may have one or two solutions for each of these income-focused investment strategies, the menu may be relatively limited, making it difficult to create a customized income-focused portfolio solely with the use of managed accounts or private asset managers.

Changing Investment Managers. In the private asset manager world, a form has to be signed by the investor and processed by the managed account department of the investment-consulting firm. Afterwards the managed account department must sell one private asset management portfolio and buy the other private asset management portfolio. This process could take a week or longer.

Why Consider Managed Accounts?

Transparency. Similar to building your own stock or bond portfolio from scratch, separately managed accounts allow investors to see, touch, and feel their portfolios. Sometimes transparency can backfire though, and investors can have a strong dislike of an individual holding or several holdings. Managed accounts have a solution for objections to individual holdings.

Socially Conscious Objection. With a private asset manager investors are often allowed to strike positions from the portfolio for socially conscious reasons, because of overlap with other personal holdings, or for any other reason. This can be beneficial for investors who are uncomfortable with a specific holding!

Taxes. As mentioned earlier, depending on the investment vehicle, an investor may not be able to exert the level of control that they desire over tax management issues. A private asset manager allows investors to have a personal cost basis in all securities, making it possible to exert more control over taxes paid on gains. In addition, private asset managers allow investors to buy and sell individual portfolio holdings for the sole purpose of offsetting gains and losses, and exercising some control of their tax situation. Typically in taxable accounts or regular accounts in excess of $1,000,000.00, investors will consider the benefits and considerations of privately managed accounts for part or all of an investment portfolio.

Cost. Managed accounts have a set fee, which in some cases can be much less than the cost of owning a variety of individual investments. One critical caveat for investors to be cognizant of *irrespective of cost* is the total performance *net of fees*. While separately managed accounts can sometimes have a cost advantage, cost cannot be looked at in a vacuum.

Investors in private asset management strategies may be able to benefit from tax control, eliminating individual holdings for socially conscious objections or other reasons, transparency of the portfolio, and potentially from cost savings. However, the higher minimums, limited menu of choices, limitation of income strategies available, and challenge of changing investment managers are potential drawbacks to owners of separately managed accounts.

V. Practice #5 Be Aware of Risk

"If you don't fail now and again, it's
a sign you're playing it safe."
WOODY ALLEN

All investors – including income investors - may face stormy investment weather. Instead of tornados, lightening, and hurricanes, income investors face inflation, deflation, credit risk, liquidity risk, tax risk, and market risk. Inflation can create **interest rate risk**, or the risk that rising rates will make current bond holdings go down in value to raise their yields to match new higher yielding bonds. Deflation can cause **reinvestment risk** or the risk that when an investor's bond matures, rates will be lower and the investor will have to reinvest at a lower rate in the future. **Credit risk** is the risk that a particular country, state, municipality, or corporation issuing a bond will default, and stop making coupon or interest payments to investors, or get downgraded in their credit rating, or go out of business, or declare bankruptcy and ultimately fail to pay back the principal amount at the stated maturity date. An additional risk income investor's face is **liquidity risk** or the risk that, if funds were needed immediately or quickly, they could not be raised without a significant cost or penalty incurred. An annuity is an example of an investment product that generates income while carrying a high degree of liquidity risk. Annuities tend to carry *liquidity risk*, with minimum holding periods required before distributing any principal value, and therefore should be used for the proper percentage of a portfolio depending upon an investor's unique profile. Investors in the higher tax brackets are often concerned with **tax risk** and the net return after taxes or in some cases the net yield, after taxes are taken into account. Finally, **market risk** is the risk that the broad stock market or bond market will decline in value, therefore reducing the price of most stocks or bonds.

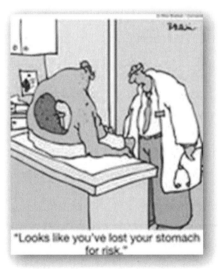

"Looks like you've lost your stomach for risk."

Licensed from www.cartoonstock.com

What are some of the ways that income investors navigate risk? In order to survive stormy and severe investment weather, income investors tend to utilize **asset allocation** as a raincoat and umbrella. While asset allocation does not keep investors completely dry, it can help to mitigate the severity of the storm. **Modern Portfolio Theory** statistics, or MPT statistics, are the weather station that can help investors to measure the risk characteristics of a portfolio. Finally, using a variety of tools an income investor can craft a **risk management strategy** that fits their investor profile!

V. A. Asset Allocation

"Data from 91 large US pension plans indicate that investment policy dominates investment strategy (market timing and security selection), explaining on average 93.6% of the variation in total plan return."

BRINSON, HOOD, GILBERT, AND BEEBOWER (1986)

How are income investors supposed to survive the thunderstorms, hurricanes, and snow storms that the markets bring? Asset allocation cannot eliminate the risk of fluctuating prices and uncertain returns. However, similar to an umbrella providing partial protection from a storm, **asset allocation** can help investors smooth out some market volatility. **Asset allocation** is the intellectual decision an investor makes to divide his or her assets up across different unique asset classes, such as stocks, bonds, and cash, and across different investment styles or sectors, such as investments that are *growth stocks* or *value* *stocks*, investments representing different capitalizations, or domestic and foreign investments, in order to help mitigate risk and smooth out returns. **Strategic asset allocation** takes place when an investor creates a portfolio with assets divided up among different asset classes and investment styles *with a long term focus*, and *rarely makes material changes* unless the (1) investor's risk profile or return goals change, (2) anticipated risk, return, or correlation of asset classes or investment styles change, or (3) a novel asset class is available that the investor did not consider earlier (Rotblut & Darst, 2012).

Rebalancing a Portfolio

One approach regarding asset allocation is the decision to allocate a portion of one's assets to asset classes or sectors that are currently out of favor and currently have little demand from investors. While this approach is not suitable for all investors and can potentially expose an investor to a substantial loss of capital, it may have merit for aggressive investors, or for the aggressive portion of one's portfolio. By making a decision to allocate assets to asset classes and sectors that currently have little interest from most investors, an investor may be able to buy into an asset class or sector at a "bargain" price. One way for investors to help ensure that they are balancing appropriate risk and reward given their investment profile is through rebalancing their portfolios. **Rebalancing** is the act of making purchases and sales in the portfolio for the sole purpose of making sure that the portfolio weightings are precisely at the proper percentages, where they were originally set when the portfolio was created, with a target risk tolerance and return goal in mind (Malkiel, 2015, pp. 359-360). For example, if a portfolio was originally 35% weighted to stocks and 65% weighted to bonds, and due to greater appreciation in the stock market over the past year the portfolio became overweighted to stocks with a 45% weighting, and underweighted to bonds with a 55% weighting, an investor would sell 10% of the portfolio out of stocks and purchase bonds, bringing the portfolio back to the original 35/65 weighting (Malkiel, 2015, pp. 359-360).

Market Timing

Some investors want to own the asset classes that are currently in vogue and performing well now, rather than practicing asset allocation and allocating among different asset classes according to their individual risk tolerance and return goals. Furthermore, investors may generally be more inclined to liquidate asset classes that are currently performing poorly. This investor behavior of attempting to buy into asset classes at the right time and sell out of asset classes at the proper time is referred to as **market timing**.

While **technical analysis**, or using charts and graphs to spot changes in market trends, can be used for market timing, many investors find that implementing a successful market timing strategy to be difficult. In contrast, by earmarking a specific percentage to different asset classes and investment styles upfront, asset allocation mitigates the need for market timing. Investors can think of asset allocation as the "antidote" to market timing.

Tactical Asset Allocation

What happens when investors combine traditional asset allocation with market timing? While it sounds heretical for an investor practicing asset allocation to utilize market timing, investors practicing **tactical asset allocation** use technical analysis and or fundamental analysis of *current market conditions* to allocate funds to different asset classes and investment styles *for more of a short term basis*, such as a year, quarter, month, or week (Rotblut & Darst, 2012). Often investors who practice *tactical asset allocation* may utilize highly liquid investments to change exposure to different asset classes rapidly (Darst, 2008, p. 30). Through professionally managed accounts, an income investor may be able to participate in an "all asset," balanced, or global allocation strategy that practices *tactical asset allocation*.

Hypothetical Retirement Income Portfolio Allocation

Stability of Principal. Many investors struggle to create a monthly retirement income similar to their former monthly paycheck, while still maintaining or growing the principal value of their asset base. The first step to develop an asset allocation plan for retirement income is for an investor to determine his or her risk tolerance, income need, and return goals, and the relative strength of each.

One important goal for some retirement income investors is stability of principal. Certificates of Deposit, various Fixed Income investments such as corporate, government or, municipal bonds, or Annuities can provide a stated return of principal while still offering income through interest or other payments for a specified period of time. Some investors will ladder these types of investments, so that the longer-term securities will provide some protection against reinvestment risk and deflation, and the shorter-term issues will provide some protection against interest rate risk and inflation.

If investors are worried about inflation they may purchase short-term fixed income securities or short duration bonds, bond portfolios, or bond mutual funds. While this method does not necessarily provide protection against deflation and reinvestment risk, it does not have a penalty like a CD or Fixed Annuity, and does protect against inflation and interest rate risk. It is important to note that asset allocation decisions are unique to each investor.

Guaranteed Income for Life. A recent survey entitled "Wells Fargo Middle Class Retirement survey" found that 22% of workers indicated they would rather die than run out of money (Kadlec, 2014)! Clearly, many retirees desire a guarantee of income for the rest of their life. While investors may purchase a variable annuity for the death benefit or tax deferred growth or capital appreciation, retirement income investors may buy variable annuities for the *guaranteed living withdrawal benefit*. A **guaranteed living withdrawal benefit** is a rider on an annuity contract that ensures the variable annuity investor income for the rest of his or her life while still being able to retain the asset and invest it for capital appreciation. This is an optional rider on a variable annuity that is available for an additional annual charge against the income base. It generally may only be selected at the time of contract purchase and cannot be changed later. It can usually be exercised only after a waiting period. Many contracts will guarantee a certain percentage for life, and may raise the amount based upon age, account performance, or both. Investors, who invest a lump sum in stocks, bonds, and other securities, have the problem of potentially running out of money due to poor performance, and have no guarantee of their retirement income for a lifetime. Variable annuities are designed to allow an investor to keep the asset for heirs and to invest for the potential of capital appreciation and for the potential of keeping up with inflation, yet also turn on a guaranteed income stream for the rest of the investor's life. Some of the challenges variable annuity investors face are a lack of total liquidity (most contracts limit the total percentage of liquidity per year) and a higher total fee structure (typically a yearly fee is charged for insurance costs and additional fees are charged for optional additional guarantees). When speaking of a Guaranteed Minimum Income Benefit associated with a Variable Annuity, it is important to consider that if this investment option is selected that the investor could incur a higher expense with the option without receiving any additional benefit. Clearly there are often positive sequences of events and positive investment outcomes over an investor's lifetime, that would not necessitate the cost of the insurance guarantee of a minimum income for the lifetime of the investor. Additionally, any guarantees are based on the claims-paying ability of the issuing insurance company. Investors must consider that the guarantees apply to minimum income from an annuity; they do not guarantee an investment return or the safety of the underlying funds. However, there are some variable annuities that have a "principal protection" rider, that do guarantee a "walk away" benefit after a stated number of years, equal to the initial investment, if the principal is less than the amount initially invested, after the pre-determined number of years.

An investor – when examining their retirement income options – will need to consider balancing out the higher fees and lower level of liquidity drawbacks of variable annuities with their three major positive attributes: (1) a guarantee of a lifetime of income, (2) the potential to keep up with inflation, and (3) the potential to leave an asset to heirs.

Maximum Flexibility. Investments that are not insurance based generally provide no guarantee of stability of principal, and no guarantee of income for life. However, these investment vehicles may be able to provide investors more flexibility of choices, a higher degree of liquidity, and typically lower expenses than variable annuities. An additional attractive feature is being able to make changes to a portfolio should the investor's portfolio objective or appetite for risk change.

An income investor can allocate across fixed annuities, variable annuities, and mutual funds or other non-insurance investment structures, in different percentages based upon his or her goals for stability of principal, guaranteed income for life, and maximum flexibility.

V. B. Risk Measurement

"More efficient investment portfolios can be
created by diversifying among asset categories
with low to negative correlations."
Dr. Harry M. Markowitz, Nobel Prize Economist

Standard Deviation

Is your portfolio or a particular security, mutual fund, privately managed account, or ETF you own, swinging wildly up and down, like a rollercoaster? Is your investment static and not moving much at all, like a parked car? **Standard deviation** is one of the most commonly used risk metrics for investments. It measures the variation from a designated average (such as annual returns) and is used to measure risk when discussing a portfolio of stocks, bonds, mutual funds, ETFs, or securities. Generally speaking, the more variation or dispersion from the mean, the more volatility that is implied, and the higher the risk the portfolio or security is assuming.

Modern Portfolio Theory (MPT) Statistics

Alpha, *beta*, *r squared* sounds like a fraternity that held spectacular keg parties when I was in college. However, rather than representing three Greek letters, these are three different types of MPT statistics. They are utilized to measure portfolio risk, or more specifically to assess the risk adjusted performance, the market sensitivity, and the correlation relative to a stock market index or another benchmark.

Beta. Beta is a measure of the risk of an investment arising from movements of the market, and measures how much a particular port-folio or security swings or moves relative to the stock market or bond market as a whole (Malkiel, 2015, p. 210). A *beta* of 1 would imply that the security or portfolio tends to move up and down 100% in tan-dem with the market as a whole. A *beta* of .5 would imply that – if the market were to rise or fall 5% - this security's return would rise or fall 2.5%. A *beta* of zero would imply a security's return is not correlated to the market. A negative beta would imply a security or portfolio tends to move in the opposite direction from the market (Hallman & Rosenbloom, 2015, pp. 72-73). All else being equal, income or retire-ment focused investors typically want more consistent returns and a relatively lower beta. However, if a beta is too low, returns will most likely suffer. For example, money markets and similar short term cash alternatives tend to have very low beta statistics relative to the S&P 500 benchmark index (S&P 500 Index (SPX) – Arguably the most widely followed and well known benchmark for tracking large US publicly traded companies. The index is comprised of 500 stocks and represents about 80% of the value of all large capitalization stocks. This is the index that is most often used as a proxy for "the market" or the "US stock market." (http://us.spindices.com/indices/equity/sp-500, 2015), but also tend to have very low returns as well! A low beta does not necessarily mean a portfolio or security can be categorized as low risk. For example, while gold generally moves "independently" from the stock market, and historically has had a zero beta (relative to the S&P 500 benchmark index), or has been considered a near zero beta asset, it can often be quite volatile, swinging up and down sharply in value, and it tends to have a high standard deviation.

The Capital Asset Pricing Model. The Capital Asset Pricing Model is used to help investors determine a theoretically appropriate rate of return on a security if it were to be added to an existing portfolio that is already diversified. According to the **capital asset pricing model (CAPM)**, the greater the systemic risk, or **beta**, is for a portfolio or security, the greater the expected return is for a portfolio or security (Malkiel, 2015, p. 216). While un-systemic risk, or risk particular to one specific stock can be diversified away by holding many stocks in a portfolio, *beta*, or systemic risk, cannot (Malkiel, 2015, p.213).While many studies have criticized CAPM for focusing solely on *beta*, and no other factors such as market capitalization, dividends, or valuation metrics, the CAPM has been useful for measuring risk and predicting returns, as one factor in the totality of the circumstances (Malkiel, 2015, pp.221-225).

Alpha. Alpha is a statistic that measures *risk adjusted* performance by measuring *how much excess return* in percentage terms did a portfolio, or single security achieve, *given the level of market risk it assumed*, or given its *beta* relative to the market (Malkiel, 2015, p. 219). For example, a portfolio that has a positive alpha of 3%, on average, for the last ten years is a portfolio that achieved, on average an excess return of 3% per year, given the level of market risk, or *beta*, the portfolio assumed. Sometimes alpha is viewed as a report card, or metric, to determine how well a portfolio manager is performing relative to his or her peer group on a risk adjusted basis.

R-Squared. Does your portfolio move up and down with the market in tandem, like a jellyfish moving up and down at the mercy of the waves of the ocean? **R-Squared** is another risk measurement tool that measures to what extent a portfolio or security is *correlated* to the stock market or bond market, or the percentage of a portfolio's movements that can be accounted for by movements of the market or benchmark index (Neubert, Bogle, & Malkiel, 2013, pp. 206-207; Hallman & Rosenbloom, 2015, p.73). Typically the S&P 500 will be used for the stock market, but any index could be used. For example if you wanted to compare a private asset manager who specialized in selecting international stocks, it may make sense to use something like the MSCI EAFE, or Europe Australasia Far East index, to determine *r-squared* since the MSCI EAFE is an unmanaged group of securities widely regarded by investors to be representative of the stock markets of Europe, Australasia and the Far East. {MSCI (EAFE) Europe Australasia Far East Index: Often recognized as the most commonly used benchmark to track foreign stock performance. It is comprised of both large and mid-cap stocks in "1st world" or developed countries located in Europe, Australasia and the Far East. It does not include the United States or Canada (https://www. msci.com/eafe, 2015).}R-squared values will range from 0 – 100, with 100 signifying that 100% of the securities movements are explained by the correlating movements in the benchmark index. By utilizing MPT statistics, investors can measure the relative risk of a single security or a portfolio of securities, relative to others and relative to any market benchmark, such as the S&P 500 or the Barclays Capital Aggregate Bond Index.{Barclays Capital Aggregate Bond Index: Widely followed broad US investment grade bond index that is "market capitalization weighted" and includes primarily corporate bonds, mortgage backed bonds, Treasuries, and Government Agency bonds in direct proportion to their size in the US investment grade bond market. The index was originally established in 1973 and was referred to as the "Lehman Aggregate Bond Index." (https://en.wikipedia.org/ wiki/Barclays_Capital_Aggregate_Bond_Index, 2015)} While *alpha*, *beta*, *r-squared*, and *standard deviation* are not the only MPT statistics used by investors, they are some of the most common.

V. C. Risk Management

"As with all investments, what you buy depends
on how much risk you can tolerate."

JAMES DINES

Risks Investors Face

Investors face many minefields while battling the markets. As we discussed earlier, bond investors face inflation and *interest rate risk*, as well as deflation and *reinvestment risk*. Assuming bond investors can handle those risks, they still have to be concerned with *credit risk* of the bond issuer as well!

Annuities carry *liquidity risk*, where if an investor sells an annuity before the term, or minimum holding period, has expired, he or she has to pay a penalty. Often it is a 1% charge for each year left of the fixed annuity term. In the case of a variable annuity, typically 10% can be liquidated each year without any penalty, and there is a 1% charge levied for distributions in excess of the 10% threshold for every year left on the minimum holding period required, which is typically four years, but could be much longer. Using annuities only for a portion of a portfolio can mitigate some of the liquidity risk.

When investors purchase stocks they face *market risk*, or the risk that the stock market will decline due to poor earnings, a decline in the general economy, conflicts in the Middle East, or other adverse political or economic events. When the stock market declines, typically three out of every four stocks will decline in sympathy with the market (Investors.com, 2015). If an investor has a concentrated position in one stock, he or she faces the *un-systemic risk*, or single stock risk, that some unforeseen event or poor earnings report could severely hurt the stock's price, irrespective of the performance of the stock market as a whole. All else being equal, investors should typically hold no more than 10% (10% to 20% according to FINRA) in any one stock holding, especially income investors and investors in or near retirement (finra.org, 2015). This general "rule of thumb," was recently "ratified" by David Blanchett, head of retirement research for Morningstar Investment Management, who advocates that investors allocate a maximum of 10% or less of their 401K plan to "company stock"(Rothman, 2013).

Tax risk is the risk that investor returns will be significantly reduced after taxes are taken into consideration. Tax risk can eat away at portfolio returns. Utilizing low turnover investment strategies can potentially mitigate taxes, by allowing investments to grow without realizing immediate capital gains. However, capital gains taxes will be incurred if the securities are eventually sold at a profit. For mutual funds, it is important to research whether a fund has a large amount of embedded capital gain exposure. In addition, private asset managers can mitigate taxes for substantial taxable investment portfolios by giving investors their own personal cost basis on each individual security, making it impossible for investors to pay taxes on gains they did not personally receive. As discussed earlier, it is possible for mutual fund investors to end up paying taxes on gains they did not personally receive. Another common method of lowering tax bills is investing in tax-free municipal bonds, or tax deferred fixed or variable annuities.

Risk Management Tools

Hedging a portfolio with put options. What if an income investor is concerned about his or her dividend paying stocks, other equity investments, and convertibles being susceptible to market declines? How can an investor help preserve some of the principal value of his or her stock portfolio? An investor who feels as if a particular index is going to decline can purchase put options on the index in direct proportion to the market risk, or *beta*, inherent in his or her portfolio, to help hedge out *market risk*, or protect against market declines. By purchasing a put option an investor obtains the right but not the obligation to sell a stock or ETF at a specified price (the **strike**

price) over a defined period of time (from the time of purchase until option expiration), in return for paying a premium.

Let's apply the same principal to a hypothetical investor's stock portfolio of $100,000.00. Let's imagine that the ETF that follows the benchmark stock index, that is the most similar to the investor's stock portfolio, is currently trading around $120. Each option contract represents 100 shares. Therefore if an investor wanted to protect $100,000.00 of his or her portfolio, they would need 8 put contracts. ($100,000.00 portfolio /(100 shares x $120.00 per share)) = 8 put contracts. This strategy should only be employed by investors who are familiar with the risks of option trading and for whom options are suitable as part of their investment strategy.

Inverse ETFs. Another way to hedge a portfolio is to buy *inverse ETFs*. An **inverse ETF** is an exchange traded fund that is designed to decline in value at times when the market advances and advance at times when the market declines. Rather than jumping in and out of the market, or utilizing options with a limited time window, some investors may allocate a percentage of their portfolio to an inverse ETF for the purpose of hedging their portfolio from market declines. While ETFs do require a greater amount of capital outlay, they do not have a limited window of time before expiration, as options do. *Inverse ETFs* are now available with two and three times leverage. As mentioned earlier, while leverage can provide greater returns, it also comes with much greater risk, and therefore lever-aged inverse ETFs typically are inappropriate for income investors.

Zero Cost Collar. Many investors take on the risk of a concen-trated stock position where a significant part, if not most, of their net worth is tied up in a single stock. The *un-systemic risk* of a single stock, or the risk that is unique to a particular stock, is often not ap-preciated until it is too late. By buying a protective put while writing an out-of-the-money covered call option at a strike price where the premium received is equivalent to the amount of premium needed to purchase the protective put is called a **zero cost collar** (Speth, 2015, pp.10-11). When appropriate, this strategy of limiting the un-systemic risk of a single stock with a *zero cost collar* can come into play when an investor is holding a high percentage of their investment portfolio in one particular stock.

Non-Correlation. By utilizing asset classes and investment styles that are not closely correlated to one another, investors can attempt to reduce overall portfolio risk, without fully com-promising return (Malkiel, 2015, pp. 196-200). Harry Markowitz, the founding father of asset allocation and MPT, first articulated this corollary (Malkiel, 2015, pp. 196-197). Gold is considered a *zero beta* asset class, because it has very little market sensitiv-ity relative to the S&P 500 benchmark index (Morningstar Fund Investor, 2014). In addition, it has a very low *r-squared*, and has little correlation to the stock market. It moves fairly independently of the market, and therefore provides excellent non-correlation. There are many examples of non-correlated assets that exist today. For example, municipal bonds also have little correlation to the stock market. In addition, foreign bonds have virtually no correlation to the US stock market. Treasury bonds have a somewhat inverse correlation to the market, and tend to go up when the market drops and fall when the market rises. Furthermore, REITs, Utilities, and Commodities all have relatively low correlations to the stock market as well. An investor can choose whether or not to add asset classes with varying amounts of correlation to the stock market as a whole to his or her portfolio, depending upon one's goals and tolerance for risk.

Market Neutral, Long-Short Equity, and Global Allocation Strategies. Another method of harnessing non-correlation to hedge against market risk in a portfolio is to utilize private asset managers or mutual funds that are *market neutral*, or have *long-short equity*, or *global allocation* strategies.

Imagine if you were to go to a football game and bet on both football teams to win. It seems sort of pointless, with each bet cancelling the other's impact. While at first glance a *market neutral* strategy also seems like it will have no impact or significant return, this strategy can be very effective. **Market Neutral** is a strategy where the private asset manager, mutual fund manager, or hedge fund manager buys stocks that he or she finds attractive and sells short the stocks that he or she finds to hold less promise. While the manager is betting on both sides, the fund or portfolio has potential to make profits regardless of which way the market is trending based upon good security selection. **Selling short** is a technique by which the manager borrows shares of stock to sell at the current market price with the hopes of buying them at a cheaper price in the future and profiting from the difference between the price the shares were sold at and the lower price they were later bought back at.

Market Neutral strategies are available in many forms including mutual funds, private asset managers, and hedge funds. Some market neutral funds are more income oriented, and write or sell covered call options to generate extra income. Income investors tend to have portfolios heavily weighted in bonds. Market Neutral strategies allow for some additional weighting outside of bonds, without taking on the full risk of stocks. Market Neutral strategies tend to have a very low standard deviation, low r-squared, and a very low beta relative to the stock market.

Long-short equity strategies are similar to market neutral strategies, except they have the ability to overweight or underweight their net market exposure, versus taking a neutral stance on the market. They tend to come in mutual fund, hedge fund, and private asset manager form. Like their close cousin, the market neutral strategy, they allow investors to diversify more and provide an additional non-correlated asset for the purpose of lowering overall portfolio risk. Long-short equity strategies tend to be less income oriented and therefore are not utilized as commonly among income investors for the core of a portfolio, but typically will be used occasionally as a hedge for a portfolio.

Managed Futures typically invest in highly liquid contracts and options that provide the right to buy or sell a traded product, financial instrument, index, currency, precious metal or commodity at a specified price, delivered on a future date. While these funds have shown significant non-correlation to the major bond and stock market averages, they tend to produce little or no income, and most come in hedge fund form with higher fees, minimum net worth requirements, and longer lock up periods. It is important to note that futures trading, which is speculative and volatile and involves a high degree of risk, and often a high degree of leverage, is only appropriate for the risk capital portion of a portfolio. Since investments in managed futures are speculative and involve substantial risk, they typically are not suitable for all investors. Investors should be aware that such investments can quickly lead to large losses as well as gains. Additionally, restrictions on redemptions may affect an investor's ability to withdraw their participation. Further, there may be substantial fees and expenses. Investors should see the disclosure documents for a complete description of investment objectives, risks, charges, and expenses. Similar to long short equity funds, investors may utilize a certain weighting to managed futures as a hedge for a portfolio.

Balanced Strategies and Global Allocation Funds. Balanced **strategies**, are strategies that invest in both stock and bonds, typically with the flexibility to move from a 50/50 stock to bond ratio to a 60/40 stock to bond ratio in either direction. They tend to pay out a consistent level of income. The bonds tend to provide income and help mute volatility, while the stocks have the potential for growth and income. By utilizing high yield bonds or lower rated investment grade bonds, managers can provide the potential for capital appreciation with the bond component of the balanced fund as well. Keep in mind that high-yield bonds, commonly known as junk bonds, are subject to greater loss of principal and interest, including default risk, than higher-rated investment grade bonds. This may result in greater share price volatility.

Global Allocation funds or **All Asset funds** can have a capital preservation focus and an "open" or "go anywhere" flexible investment mandate, with the ability to hold cash, stocks, bonds, commodities, REITs, utilities, convertibles, emerging market stocks and bonds, foreign stocks and bonds, gold, and treasury inflation protected securities, to name a few. They often have the ability to buy puts, use margin, or hold large cash positions as well.

Risk Management for Bond Investors

Investing in fixed income securities involves certain risks such as market risk if sold prior to maturity and credit risk especially if investing in high yield bonds, which have lower ratings and are subject to greater volatility. All fixed income investments may be worth less than original cost upon redemption or maturity therefore, even though bonds may carry a notion of percieved safety with investors, it is important to address risk management when investing in bonds.

Dynamic or Strategic Bond Investing. Traditionally investors would purchase a *bond ladder*, staggering the maturity of different bond issues over different intervals of time, usually annually or quarterly, for the purpose of having long-term bonds to help hedge against deflation or reinvestment risk, and short-term bonds to help protect against inflation and interest rate risk. Of course, Bond laddering does not assure a profit or protect against loss in a declining market.

Bill Gross, the famous billionaire bond portfolio manager, was the first manager to make popular the notion that investors can manage a bond portfolio and make more money by trading bonds, rather than laddering out the maturity dates uniformly. Today, many bond managers are like Bill Gross, and run strategic income portfolios where they can "game the economic cycle." They buy speculative debt, in anticipation of the economy improving, or as the economy is improving and GDP is growing, and bonds are receiving credit upgrades, causing the bonds to appreciate in price.

In addition, strategic income portfolio managers will buy long term high quality debt in anticipation of challenging economic times, or during challenging economic times and periods where GDP is contracting, when interest rates are declining, because long term high quality bonds are the most interest rate sensitive, and will move inversely with interest rate movements, appreciating in price in a declining interest rate environment. A move into high quality bonds will help protect against credit risk as well. Similarly, strategic bond managers will buy floating rate bonds and treasury inflation protected securities when they believe they can capitalize on a rising interest rate environment, where the bonds will pay more and appreciate in price as rates rise.

In addition, dynamic or multi-sector bond managers will purchase foreign bonds that take advantage of currency movements and different interest rate cycles. Bond managers that select foreign bonds look for countries with more fiscal discipline than the United States and faster growing GDP than the US, with the hopes of making money on the appreciation of the foreign currency against the dollar. Furthermore, when GDP is growing, strategic bond managers may buy convertible bonds, higher yielding bonds, and short-term bonds or short duration bonds to protect against interest rate risk and inflation. Investors can utilize any of the specific strategies mentioned above as separate individual strategies as well.

Income investors clearly face a great deal of risk, but there are significant risk management tools and strategies investors can utilize to mitigate investment risk, yet not to eliminate it.

VI. Practice #6 Relate to Case Studies of Income Investors

"I read true crime books, and I read when people do
case studies of stuff. I'm into books like that. Case
studies or forensics or murder - all that good stuff."

TOM ARAYA

We have discussed at length the major tools or asset classes, investment styles, and investment strategies that income investors have in their toolbox to create income and still keep up with inflation. However, when are investors supposed to use each tool? What dosage or percentage of a portfolio is appropriate for each tool or asset class, investment style, or strategy? Under what types of market conditions, investor circumstances, and investor objectives and risk tolerances are different investment strategies and allocations appropriate? While it may not be as exciting and mysterious as the true crime books and forensics quoted above, *case studies of income investors* can help us answer these questions!

Once income investors determine their risk tolerance and investment goals, then they can craft a comprehensive investment strategy. While there are many standard questionnaires used by advisors, investment firms and investors to assess one's risk tolerance and investment goals, the following is an example of a questionnaire:

1. On a 1 to 10 scale, where one is the most conservative investor and 10 is the most aggressive investor, where do you fall on the spectrum of risk tolerance for investing? (Answer between 1 and 10)

2. In the next five years, how stable would you consider your current and future income sources?

   _ Very Stable

   _ Stable

   _ Unstable

   _ Very Unstable

3. What is your total household income including earned and investment income?

   _ Less than $100,000

   _ $100,000 to $499,999

_ $500,000 to $999,999

_ $1,000,000 +

4. This investment will represent what percentage of your total investment assets?

    _ Less than 20%

    _ 21% to 50%

    _ 51% to 75%

    _ 76% to 100%

5. When it comes to investing in stocks, bonds, mutual funds, or ETF's, would you describe yourself as_____.

    _ Very Inexperienced

    _ Inexperienced

    _ Experienced

    _ Very Experienced

    Years of Experience: _____

6. If the market were to suffer a major drawdown, what is the maximum percentage that your portfolio could suffer *in negative performance*, without you becoming extremely uncomfortable and wanting to cash out of the portfolio and abandon your asset aliocation plan and your investment plan?

    _ < 10%

    _ 10% to 25%

_ 25% to 50%

_ > 50%

7. What is your current age?

_ Under 35

_ Between 36 and 45

_ Between 46 and 55

_ Between 56 and 70

_ Over 70

8. What is your time frame for this investment?

_ Immediate (Less than 3 years)

_ Short Term (3-5 years)

_ Moderate Term (5-10 years)

_ Long Term (10+ years)

9. Which option best describes your risk tolerance?

_ Less accepting of risk – Conservative

_ Accepting some degree of risk

_ Moderate

_ More accepting of risk – Long Term

10. Are you open to international investments? (Yes or no)

11. Do you have any socially conscious objections, such as tobacco, alcohol, firearms, or other sin stocks?

12. While investors seek the dual goals of relatively high returns and stability of principal, if you had to lean one way or the

other which goal is more paramount? (Relatively high returns or stability of principal?)

13. Intuitively, what percentage of your portfolio would you like to be in bonds or fixed income securities?

14. Keeping in mind that the higher the "average annual hypothetical projected return" the greater the likelihood of negative performance in some years and the greater likelihood of larger drawdowns, what type of long term investment return in average percentage terms (over a 3, 5, and 10 year plus time frame), would you like to achieve?

    _ Average Annual Hypothetical Projected Return of 3%

    _ Average Annual Hypothetical Projected Return of 4%

    _ Average Annual Hypothetical Projected Return of 6%

    _ Average Annual Hypothetical Projected Return of 8%

15. Are you retired or still working? If still working, when are you retiring?

16. What is your primary goal for your investments? Secondary goal? (Place a "1" and a "2" next to the appropriate goal)

    _ Provide Current Income

    _ Preservation of Wealth

    _ Fund Retirement

    _ Build Long-Term Wealth

17. Which of the following best describes your current income needs?

    _ None – Not expecting any need for income, the primary objective of the portfolio should be growth

    _ Some – Income from the portfolio is needed, but willing to accept a lower level of income for the potential of long-term returns

    _ Moderate – Need for a moderate level of income including interest and dividends.

    _ Significant – Primary investment goal is income. Willing to accept less potential for long – term returns in order to seek higher income.

18. Is the investment to be made in an account subject to taxation or a tax deferred or *qualified* retirement plan?

Often investors will struggle with many of the above questions, not wanting to give the wrong answer. The questions are tough because they force investors to make decisions on what type of investor they are, and while it is not realistic, it is human nature to want high investment returns with low risk! While many of the above risk tolerance and investment goal questions overlap, and investors will sometimes have conflicting answers, or answers that are not realistic given other answers, it is important for an investor or investment advisor to weigh answers appropriately, in the context of all the other answers, when crafting an asset allocation and investment plan.

Let's take a look at some hypothetical case studies. The studies are based upon actual investors, a combination of actual investors, or in some cases, in whole or in part, hypothetical investors, who had a primary objective of income investing! The studies range the gamut from conservative, to moderately conservative, to moderate, to moderately aggressive, to aggressive. It is important to note that the solutions discussed may not be suitable for your personal situation, even if it is similar to the example presented. Investors should make their own decisions based on their specific investment objectives and financial circumstances. It should not be assumed that the recommendations made in this situation achieved any of the goals mentioned. These examples are hypothetical and do not represent any specific investments or strategies, rather general information to help put in perspective and context some of the investing for income concepts and strategies discussed earlier.

Licensed from www.cartoonstock.com

VI. A. Case Study of the Conservative Income Investor

"I'm not as interested in return on my principal as I am return of my principal."

WILL ROGERS

We have all heard stories about friends, relatives or neighbors that would take their savings and bury them in the backyard during the Great Depression! While one would think the public's distrust of banks and investments is different in modern times, in October of 2008, during the recent credit crises, *Sentry Safe* reported that sales of safes were up approximately 70% year over year (Philipp, 2008)!

While conservative investors may not be hiding their funds in the backyard like during the Great Depression, they are looking to take only the bare minimum of risk, in exchange for a modest return. Client A is a 78-year old retired widow who lives on a taxable portfolio of $500,000.00 in CDs, which have matured for the most part, farm income, and social security.

Client A described herself, as a 2/3 on an investment risk tolerance scale, where 1 is the most conservative investor and 10 is the most aggressive investor. She mentioned that her husband owned stocks, bonds, and mutual funds at times in the past, but she "never followed the markets." She mentioned she could only withstand about a few percentage points of downside risk, but she understood that investments outside of CDs and fixed annuities would fluctuate in value and returns were not guaranteed. Furthermore she felt she should have 100% of her money in bonds, was open to international investments, and she valued stability of principal over relatively high returns. She understood the concept that investing in fixed income securities involves certain risks such as market risk if sold prior to maturity and credit risk (especially if investing in high yield bonds). Speculative-grade fixed income securities have lower credit ratings and are subject to greater volatility. She also understood that all fixed income investments may be worth less than the original cost paid upon redemption or the maturity of the bond. Additionally, she mentioned that she didn't want to "have to pay a lot in taxes," and she was looking for about a 3% return. Finally, Client A mentioned that she would like a monthly check sent to her for the income but she wanted to "keep the principal invested."

Historically, a typical "conservative income" asset allocation is comprised of approximately 80% bonds and 20% to other investments.

Based on her age, her other investments, investment experience, financial situation and needs, tax status, investment objectives, investment experience, investment time horizon, liquidity needs, and risk tolerance a conservative income allocation is appropriate for Client A.

A hypothetical portfolio for Client A may be allocated as follows:

- 5% dedicated to cash or cash alternatives,
- 75% allocated to traditional, investment grade fixed income products of varying maturities (short term, intermediate and long term),
- 15% allocated to alternative income sources (these may include things such as international or emerging market debt, REITs, and/or high yield investments)
- 5% allocated to equities.

Let's take a closer look at the allocation to traditional, investment grade bonds. Since Client A is a resident of the State of Kansas and has expressed a tax-related concern, she may want to consider a portfolio of investment grade Kansas municipal bonds because the portfolio will pay her income that is exempt from federal and state taxes. Keep in mind that – while the interest income is tax-free – any capital gains will be subject to taxes and, for some investors, the income may be subject to the Alternative Minimum Tax. Since municipal bonds are non-correlated to equities, they should have little fluctuation with the ups and downs of the stock market. In addition, they are typically less sensitive to interest rates than taxable bonds, and are typically relatively stable in price. In order to help protect against rising interest rates and inflation, she should consider allocating a portion of the fixed income portfolio to short-term bonds. Moving onto the alternative income allocation, she may want to consider investments such as international fixed income, REITs, and emerging market debt or high-yield bonds to create her desired income stream.

Now let's take a closer look at the stock portion of the allocation. Since Client A is a conservative income investor, she may want to consider an allocation to large and mid-cap stocks of established corporations that have historically paid a dividend to help provide an income stream. She would need to consider the possibility that the dividend is not guaranteed and could be raised or eliminated without notice. An allocation to international stocks may be appropriate as well for diversification purposes. (Keep in mind that diversification cannot guarantee a profit in a declining market, and that investing in foreign securities presents certain risks not associated with domestic investments, such as currency fluctuation, political and economic instability, and different accounting standards. This may result in greater share price volatility.)

VI. B. Case Study of the Moderate Income Investor

"Some studies show that women can be better money managers than men because they tend to be more conservative and do their homework. Men tend to take more risks without the research."

MARIA BARTIROMO

The moderate income investor understands that in order to achieve higher returns than cash or cash alternatives, he or she must take on additional risk, including a more significant exposure to stock market risk. Unlike the conservative income investor, the moderate income investor may be able to accept a higher degree of illiquidity for part of a portfolio. In addition, he or she is typically receptive to some level of stock market exposure, and utilizing strategies that are designed to control some of this risk.

Let's take a look at an income investor who is a moderate income investor. Client B just retired from a national accounting firm and wanted to roll over both her ESOP (employee stock ownership plan) and her 401(k) to an IRA, stating that she wanted to be able to choose from a wider array of investments and create a customized income portfolio that she could live off of for the rest of her life in retirement. The total value of the 401(k) and the ESOP is $2 million. She has no pensions and no investments outside of her company ESOP and 401(k) retirement plan. Social security of $36,000.00 a year is her only other source of retirement income. She is used to living on $150,000.00 a year in gross income, but is willing to live on "10% less" during retirement. One of her concerns is leaving behind assets to her children.

After reconciling Client B's answers with one another, Client B was determined to fall squarely in the "moderate income" category of investors. On a scale of 1 to 10, where 1 is the most conservative investor and 10 is the most aggressive investor, she described herself as a "3/4". She said she could take on approximately a 10% drawdown of her portfolio, during a major bear market, without becoming alarmed to the point of wanting to cash out. She envisioned a majority of her money in bonds or fixed income. She opted for stability of principal as a primary goal over the goal of high returns. Just like Client A, she understood the concept that investing in fixed income securities involves certain risks such as market risk if sold prior to maturity and credit risk (especially if investing in high yield bonds). Speculative-grade debt is associated with investing in fixed income securities with lower credit ratings and therefore it is subject to greater volatility. She also understood that all fixed income investments may be worth less than the original cost paid upon redemption or the maturity of the bond. As far as preferences go, she was open to international investments, recognizing that they present certain unique risks not associated with domestic investments, such as currency fluctuation and political and economic changes which could lead to more fluctuations, and had no socially conscious objections. She mentioned that over the "long term" she was hoping to achieve an average annual investment return of approximately 4% or greater.

A hypothetical portfolio for Client B may be allocated as follows:

- 3% dedicated to cash or cash alternatives,
- 54% allocated to traditional, investment grade fixed income products of varying maturities,
- 23% allocated to alternative income sources,
- 20% allocated to equities

Let's take a look at Client B's investment portfolio. Over 50% of the portfolio is allocated to traditional fixed income products with a diverse number of holdings, a spectrum of maturities – from short term to intermediate term, to long term, and varying credit quality to combat some of the general risks of investing in bonds such as interest rate risk, inflation, market risk, unsystematic risk or company specific risk, and reinvestment risk. Client B may want to consider staggering maturities between long-term, intermediate and short-term, so that the short term bonds protect against interest rate risk and the long term bonds protect against reinvestment risk. Moving onto the alternative income allocation, she may want to consider investments such as international fixed income, REITs, emerging market debt or high-yield bonds to create her desired income stream. Now let's take a closer look at the stock portion of the allocation. Compared to the conservative income investor, Client B has a larger allocation to this asset class. Since Client B is a moderate income investor, she may want to consider an allocation to small and mid-cap stocks as well as a portion to large cap stocks of established corporations that have historically paid a dividend to help provide an income stream. She would need to consider the possibility that the dividend is not guaranteed and could be raised or eliminated without notice. An allocation to international stocks may be appropriate as well for diversification purposes.

Finally, the client expressed a desire to leave a legacy to her children while still accomplishing her desire to create a customized investment portfolio and a retirement income stream. One investment she may want to consider would be a variable annuity with a living benefit rider. This would allow Client B to customize the subaccounts to reflect her investor profile while paying out a guaranteed stream of income over the course of Client B's lifetime. Since this product comes with a pro-rata death benefit, it will provide some protection of the benefits for Client B's heirs, should she pass away after a sharp decline in the stock market. It is important for investors to invest within their risk tolerance, even inside of a variable annuity, because the value should be protected 1) to leave a greater asset behind to heirs, 2) to have the chance of performance based increased annual guaranteed payouts, 3) to protect the value in case the investor wants to upgrade to a different annuity or investment upon the surrender charge expiration. A variable annuity investor like Client B must also consider that 1) Guarantees are based on the claims-paying ability of the issuing insurance company. Guarantees apply to minimum income from an annuity; they do not guarantee an investment return or the safety of the underlying subaccounts, 2) A Guaranteed Minimum Income Benefit (GMIB) feature is an optional rider on a variable annuity that is available for an additional annual charge against the income base. It generally may only be selected at the time of contract purchase and cannot be changed later. It can usually be exercised only after a waiting period. A GMIB feature is not a cash or account value. Please be advised that depending on the performance of the investment option selected, the contract value at the time of annuitization could be such that the investor would incur a higher expense with the GMIB option without receiving any additional benefit, 3) The death benefit and cash value will be affected by any outstanding loans or withdrawals at the time of surrender.

VI. C. "Everything in Moderation": Case Study of the Moderate Growth & Income Investor

"Be moderate in everything, including moderation."

HORACE PORTER

M any of the more popular media outlets and investment periodicals will tempt investors to vacillate between investing in bonds and cash and being fully invested in stocks. The moderate investor is typically more of a balanced investor, investing in both stocks and bonds. Moderate investors tend to invest close to a 50%/50% allocation of stocks to bonds.

Client C is a 48-year old high-level corporate executive at an internet coupon service company in San Francisco, California, that has just gone public. Client C lives comfortably on a $250,000.00 annual salary. He has $2 million in company stock, with a low cost basis, since he bought his shares for $5.00 a share with $100,000.00 as an initial investment prior to the public offering. Now the company stock is priced at $100.00 a share and trades at a P/E or price to earnings multiple of 75. He feels that the stock could be overvalued, because essentially the core strategy of his company is to provide coupons over the Internet that can be used locally, and his fear is that competition can easily duplicate the success of his company, driving the stock price back down! He also has $300,000.00 in cash that used to be invested in CDs in a taxable or non-retirement account. He mentioned that he is in the highest tax bracket, and when possible he would like to limit his exposure to taxes. He also mentioned that he would like more money to grow "tax deferred" like his 401(k) does.

Client C assessed his risk/reward profile as follows: On a 1 to 10 scale, with a 1 being the value awarded the most conservative investor and 10 representing the most aggressive investor, Client C falls near the middle as a "5/6." If the market were to suffer a peak to bottom decline of 40% to 60%, or more, Client C could suffer a 25% drawdown without wanting to cash out of his portfolio. While he understands that investing in foreign securities presents certain risks not associated with domestic investments, such as currency fluctuation, political and economic instability, and different accounting standards (which could result in greater share price volatility), he is open to having international or global investments, and he has no socially conscious objections. When weighing the trade-off between the two goals of high returns and stability of principal, Client C weighs both goals equally and does not lean one way or the other. He would like to achieve about a 5.5% average annual return over long periods of time. His 401(k) does not allow for in-service

withdrawals or withdrawals while he is still employed by the corporation; therefore he is only going to invest his taxable money, or his
money outside of his 401(k) retirement plan.

Based on his age, his other investments and investment experience, financial situation and needs, tax status, investment objectives,
investment time horizon, liquidity needs, and risk tolerance, a "moderate growth and income" allocation would make sense for Client C.
A hypothetical portfolio for Client C may be allocated as follows:

- 3% dedicated to cash or cash alternatives,
- 29% allocated to traditional, investment grade fixed income
  products of varying maturities,
- 18% allocated to alternative income sources,
- 2% allocated to commodities,
- 48% allocated to equities.

Let's take a look at the allocation to traditional, investment grade
bonds. Client C understands the risks – such as market risk if the
bonds are sold prior to maturity and credit risk, especially if investing in high yield bonds, which have lower ratings and are subject to
greater volatility. He knows that all fixed income investments may
be worth less than original cost upon redemption or maturity.

Given Client C's residency is the State of California and that
he has expressed a tax – related concern, he may want to consider

municipal bonds, which have a very low correlation to domestic stocks. By using a California municipal bond strategy Client C will collect income free of both federal and California State taxes. While the interest income is tax-free, capital gains, if any, will be subject to taxes. Income for some investors like Client C may be subject to the federal Alternative Minimum Tax (AMT).

In order to help protect against rising interest rates and inflation while still providing the potential for capital appreciation and income, he should consider allocating a portion of the fixed income portfolio to short-term or intermediate bonds.

Moving onto the alternative income allocation that also provides the potential for capital appreciation, he may want to consider a weighting to emerging market debt or high-yield bonds. Now let's take a closer look at the stock portion of the allocation. Since Client C is a moderate growth & income investor, he may want to consider an allocation to large cap value and growth stocks in order to help create an income stream through investing in established corporations that have historically paid a dividend while also addressing his capital appreciation needs. Client C, however, will need to account for the possibility that a dividend could be cancelled, lowered or raised without warning since they are not guaranteed. An allocation to international stocks and emerging markets stocks may be appropriate as well. In addition, he may want to allocate part of his equity position to convertible bonds which will potentially appreciate in value along with their corresponding stocks during prosperous times, yet potentially guarding against the downside risks during more challenging times, with (1) a defined coupon payment and (2) a finite value provided at a specific maturity date.

VI. D. "Push the Car Right to the Redline – But No Further!" Case Study of the Long-Term Income Investor

"My motto is: Live every day to the
fullest - in moderation."

LINDSAY LOHAN

As an investor moves toward the more aggressive end of the investment risk spectrum, he or she may overweight the allocation to stocks in their portfolio relative to the fixed income allocation in their portfolio.

Client D is a 62-year-old Engineer. He is retiring in the next 90 days, and will collect both a pension for $50,000.00 a year and social security of $30,000.00 a year. Client D "doesn't want to touch the principal" and only wants to "live off of the income generated from the portfolio." Client D hopes he can grow his portfolio, even during retirement, by investing more towards stocks, while still allowing adequate income to help fund his retirement. Furthermore he wants to withdraw only 3% or $60,000.00 per year from his

$2,000,000.00 401(k) plan, which he plans to rollover to an IRA after he retires.

Client D defines his investment risk tolerance as a "6/7" on a risk scale, where 1 is the most conservative and 10 is the most aggressive investor. In a major 40% to 60% drawdown in the stock market, Client D claims that he could withstand a 30% to 35% drawdown in his portfolio, without the need to re-allocate. He credits his fortitude during down markets to the fact that 1) he plans on only taking distributions from the cash flow of the portfolio, 2) his experience of multiple bear markets and economic cycles, and 3) the fact that he recognizes that he has to assume more risk and a more severe drawdown, on occasion, in order to achieve higher returns. Client D has no socially conscious objections, is open to foreign investing, and weighs high returns as a more primary goal than stability of principal, although stability of principal is somewhat important as well! Intuitively, Client D would like to have under 40% of his portfolio in "traditional" fixed income securities. Over the long term, Client D would like to achieve an 6.5% average annual return for the portfolio. Based on his age, his other investments and investment experience, financial situation and needs, tax status, investment objectives, investment time horizon, liquidity needs, and risk tolerance, a Long-Term Income allocation would be appropriate for Client D

A hypothetical Long-Term Income portfolio may be allocated as follows:

- 3% dedicated to cash or cash alternatives,
- 39% allocated to traditional, investment grade fixed income products of varying maturities,
- 30% allocated to alternative income sources,
- 28% allocated to equities.

Looking at this allocation, in order to address his income needs while being sensitive to factors such as inflation, he may want to consider a heavier weighting to intermediate term bonds in the traditional, investment grade fixed income category. In the alternative income allocation, while REITs and international fixed income play an important role, in order to provide income while providing the potential for capital appreciation, he may want to consider weightings that are heavier on High-yield and emerging market debt. In addition to the typical fixed income risks (market risk and the risk that the investment may be worth less than the original cost at maturity or redemption), Client D will need to be comfortable with the greater volatility associated with high-yield bonds and emerging market debt. As an investor, Client D should not place undue reliance on yield as a factor to be considered in selecting a high yield investment since high-yield bonds, also known as junk bonds, are subject to greater risk of loss of principal and interest, including default risk, than higher-rated bonds. And when it comes to investing in foreign securities there are in fact risks not associated with domestic investments - currency fluctuation, political and economic instability, and different accounting standards that could result in greater share price volatility. Ultimately, in an emerging market situation, this volatility could be heightened. Finally, a nearly equal weighting of small, mid, large and international growth and value stocks should help bolster his income stream and capital appreciation potential through purchases of established companies that historically have paid dividends, which of course are not guaranteed.

VI. E. "Roll the Dice!" – Case Study of the Long-Term Growth and Income Investor

"I haven't tried to buffer myself. I like rolling the dice."

KEVIN COSTNER

I nearly skipped the Long-Term Growth and Income Investor sub-chapter, because investing for income and investing aggressively, are seemingly at opposite ends of the investment risk spectrum. Typically income investors are looking for 1) retirement income, 2) a replacement for income, 3) a supplement to wage or earned income, 4) replacement income for a business owner from the proceeds of the business sale, or 5) a more stable portfolio. In contrast, aggressive investors typically are not concerned with the above goals, and instead are solely focused on high returns, growth, and capital appreciation.

Client E is one of those income investors who is an aggressive investor as well. Client E owns real estate, several restaurants, and has over $2,000,000.00 in individual stocks at a few investment firms. The income from his restaurants and real estate covers several multiples of his living expenses. Although he can be a very speculative investor at times since he is always looking for "hot stocks", or stocks that he feels have tremendous appreciation potential, he also likes to get paid while he waits for the stocks potentially to appreciate in price and he would like a measure of income generation in his portfolio.

As far as Client E's risk/return profile goes, he describes himself as an aggressive investor or a speculative investor. On a scale of 1 to 10, where one is the most conservative and 10 is the most aggressive, he considers himself an "8/9." When asked what type of portfolio drawdown he could take, without being uncomfortable or wanting to cash out, he stated, "75% or greater." Client E added that he has "ridden things down to zero before." That's the cry of the aggressive investor! Client E mentioned that he wants a large percentage of his portfolio in stocks but that he would also like some income even though he understands that it could be less than if he were to go with a higher weighting to traditional fixed income and alternative income allocations. He has no socially conscious objections, is open to international investments, and prefers high returns hands down to stability of principal, as far as goals go.

Based on his age, his other investments and investment experience, financial situation and needs, tax status, investment objectives, investment time horizon, liquidity needs, and risk tolerance, a "Long-Term Growth & Income" allocation may be appropriate for Client E. He would like to achieve a return of 7% long term.

A hypothetical Long-Term Growth & Income portfolio may be allocated as follows:

- 3% dedicated to cash or cash alternatives,
- 11% allocated to traditional, investment grade fixed income products of varying maturities (short term, intermediate and long term),
- 21% allocated to alternative income sources,
- 65% allocated to equities.

Looking at this allocation, in order to address his income needs while being sensitive to factors such as inflation, he may want to consider a heavier weighting to intermediate term bonds in the traditional, investment grade fixed income category. In the alternative income allocation, while REITs and international fixed income play an important role, in order to provide some income while providing the potential for capital appreciation, he may want to consider a weighting that is heavier on High-yield and emerging market debt. Since he has a more "aggressive" investment objective than other income investors, he is comfortable with the standard risks associated with investing in fixed income (market risk and the risk that the investment may be worth less than the original price at redemption) and is clear that high-yield bonds are subject to greater risk of loss of principal and interest, including default risk, than higher-rated bonds. Just like with the high-yield bonds, he is comfortable with the fact that currency fluctuation, political and economic instability, and different accounting standards could result in greater share price volatility when it comes to international investments. Finally, a weighting that is heavy on the Large Cap Growth and Large Cap Value stocks that is integrated with an allocation of small, mid, international and emerging market stocks should help bolster his income stream and his capital appreciation potential through purchases of established companies that historically have paid dividends.

Conclusion

"This is the end, beautiful friend
This is the end, my only friend
The end of our elaborate plans
The end of everything that stands
The end."
JIM MORRISON OF THE DOORS –
"THE END" FROM "THE DOORS" ALBUM

Licensed from www.cartoonstock.com

Today, income investors have a wide choice of toppings, or income-generating investment strategies, to place on top of their pizza pie, or income-focused portfolio of different slices of asset classes and investment styles. Similar to the cartoon above, today's income investors can order their "pension with everything on it!" Income investors are not limited to low yielding CDs and money market rates. Multiple bond, annuity, and stock strategies can be employed to create an income stream for investors. While different investment vehicles and combinations of investment vehicles can be utilized, investors seeking diversification and *different levels of* professional management have a wide variety of choices in the current market.

Understanding asset allocation, risk, risk measurement, and risk management strategies helps income investors balance the desire for income and moderate capital appreciation with the need to limit portfolio risk. We can put different asset classes, investment styles, risk, and investment structures in greater context by examining Case Studies or examples of investment solutions for income investors with different types of risk/reward profiles.

This book serves as a basic introduction to income investing and **does not constitute individual investment advice, tax advice, or legal advice**. It is important for investors to work with an advisor or do additional research to determine the best comprehensive investment strategy to meet their unique needs.

I still remember over 10 years ago, I asked a client how he selected his asset allocation plan for his 401(k) plan at work. He said that his cubicle neighbor read the *Wall Street Journal* and therefore he chose his selection to precisely mirror his neighbor's. I explained that there is no single right way to allocate a portfolio, but it must be *customized* to your particular situation and therefore it is not advisable to copy your co-worker's allocation. It is important that income investors determine the right allocation of investments based upon their unique risk profile, goals for income, goals for return, age, pension income, social security income, desired standard of living, and other unique factors.

THE END

References
Indices Defined

Market Index: The total value of a group of stocks, bonds, or other investment vehicles that is used as a benchmark to measure positive and negative changes in markets. (The market indices below are ones referred to in this book.) (http://www.investopedia.com/terms/m/marketindex.asp, 2015).

Barclays Capital Aggregate Bond Index: Widely followed broad US investment grade bond index that is "market capitalization weighted" and includes primarily corporate bonds, mortgage backed bonds, Treasuries, and Government Agency bonds in direct proportion to their size in the US investment grade bond market. The index was originally established in 1973 and was referred to as the "Lehman Aggregate Bond Index" (https://en.wikipedia.org/wiki/Barclays_Capital_Aggregate_Bond_Index, 2015).

Bloomberg US Corporate Bond Index: A diversified bond index created by Bloomberg for the purpose of creating a benchmark for tracking the changes in value and yield of United States investment grade corporate bonds. As of October 29, 2015, the index had the following relevant characteristics: "yield to maturity" of 3.37%, "effective duration" of 7.04, "average life" of 10.49, and the number of issues that comprise the diversified index is 5,543 (http://www.bloomberg.com/quote/BUSC:IND, 2015).

BVAL Municipal Benchmark 5 Year Index: A diversified US tax exempt AAA (average credit quality from Moody's and S&P) municipal bond index created by Bloomberg for the purpose of creating a benchmark for tracking the changes in value and yield of 5 year municipal bonds. Bloomberg uses data from the Municipal Securities Rulemaking Board, new issue calendars, and other proprietary sources (http://www.bloomberg.com/quote/BVMB5Y:IND, 2015).

Consumer Price Index (CPI): This index is a widely followed index used to track inflation in the economy. It tracks monthly figures for prices for a set of goods and services purchased by urban consumers. The index is maintained by the United States Department of Labor Bureau of Labor Statistics. Yields on some inflation indexed

bonds, social security payment increases, and retirement contributions are all determined by changes in "CPI" (http://www.bls.gov/
cpi/, 2015).

London Interbank Offered Rate (LIBOR): a common benchmark
interest rate that is used by banks and financial institutions to make
changes to adjustable rate mortgages, financial instruments, business
loans, as well as floating rate lines of credit. The acronym stands
for "London Interbank Offered Rate" and is determined by using
rates that banks charge each other for short term loans (http://www.
bankrate.com/rates/interest-rates/libor.aspx, 2015; http://www.
investopedia.com/terms/l/libor.asp, 2015).

MSCI (EAFE) Europe Australasia Far East Index: Often recognized
as the most commonly used benchmark to track foreign stock performance. It is comprised of both large and mid-cap stocks in "1st
world" or developed countries located in Europe, Australasia and the
Far East. It does not include the United
States or Canada (https://www.msci.com/eafe, 2015).

S&P 500 Index (SPX): Arguably the most widely followed and well
known benchmark for tracking large US publicly traded companies.
The index is comprised of 500 stocks and represents about 80% of

the value of all large capitalization stocks. This is the index that is most often used as a proxy for "the market" or the "US stock market" (http://us.spindices.com/indices/equity/sp-500, 2015).

References

Aneiro, M. (2014). Junk Yields: Too Low for Comfort? High prices and narrowing spreads suggest a poor long-term outlook for junk bonds. Barron's. Dow Jones & Co. Retrieved from: http://www.barrons.com/articles/SB50001424053111904742804579284782318705204

Bank, E. (2015). How do I analyze convertible bonds? Zacks. Retrieved from: http://finance.zacks.com/analyze-convertible-bonds-10395.html

Bary, E. (2015). 8 Undervalued, Large-Cap, Dividend-Paying Stocks. The Wall Street Journal. Dow Jones & Company, Inc. Retrieved from: http://www.barrons.com/articles/8-undervalued-large-cap-dividend-paying-stocks-1435640374#printMode

Benz, C. (2015). The Best Diversifier Has Been the Simplest. Despite a proliferation of diversification alternatives, high-quality bonds have provided the best antidote to equities over the past decade. Morningstar. Morningstar, Inc. Retrieved from: http://news.morningstar.com/articlenet/article.aspx?id=697751

Bigda, C. (2014). Rake in 6% with preferred stocks. Kiplinger. Retrieved from: http://www.kiplinger.com/article/investing/T052-C008-S002-rake-in-6-percent-yield-with-preferred-stocks.html

Bloomberg.com (2015, October 9th). Bloomberg Business. Markets/ Rates+Bonds/United States. US Treasury Yields & Treasury Inflation Protected Securities (TIPS).

Boitnott, J. (2015). These 7 states have no income tax—and that's not even the best part. Inc. Magazine. Mansueto Ventures LLC. New York, NY. Retrieved from: http://www.inc.com/john-boitnott/why-workers-are-moving-to-the-7-states-with-no-income-tax.html

Bojinov, S. (2015). ETFdb. 3 Simple Moving Average ETF Trading Strategies. MitreMedia. Retrieved from: http://etfdb.com/etf-trading-strategies/3-simple-moving-average-etf-trading-strategies/

Brewer, R. G. (2015). CEFs Versus Actively Managed ETFs. Seekingalpha.com. Retrieved from: http://seekingalpha.com/article/3047656-cefs-versus-actively-managed-etfs

Brinson G. P., Hood, L. R., Gilbert P., & Beebower G. P. (1986, July/August). Determinants of portfolio performance. Financial Analysts Journal, 42(4), 39-44.

Carlisle, T. (2014). Drawdowns for value versus the market in a crash: dot com bust and credit crisis. Greenbackd. Retrieved from: http://greenbackd.com/2014/05/12/drawdowns-for-value-versus-the-market-in-a-crash-dot-com-bust-and-credit-crisis/

Carnevale, C. (2015). ValueWalk. Retired with money to invest? Consider playing defense with utility stocks. Retrieved from: http://www.valuewalk.com/2015/06/retired-with-money-to-invest-consider-playing-defense-with-utility-stocks/

Darst, D. M. (2008). The art of asset allocation: Principles and investment strategies for any market (2nd ed.). New York, NY: McGraw-Hill.

Davis, J., Allaga-Diaz, R., Thomas, C. (2012). Forecasting stock returns: What signals matter, and what do they say now? Vangaurd Group Inc. Retrieved from: https://personal.vanguard.com/pdf/s338.pdf

Dow Jones & Company, Inc. (2015). How to Choose an Exchange-Traded Fund (ETF). The Wall Street Journal. Retrieved from: http://guides.wsj.com/personal-finance/investing/how-to-choose-an-exchange-traded-fund-etf/

Easterling, E. (2015). Are we there yet? Secular stock market cycle status. Crestmont Research. Retrieved from: http://www.crestmontresearch.com/docs/Stock-There-Yet.pdf

Edwards, A. (2015). Investors.com. Investors Corner. How to invest: seek innovative new companies. Retrieved from: http://education.investors.com/investors-corner/733654-how-to-invest-in-stocks.htm

Farmer, S.V. & Van Horn, Jr., J.W. (2014). In-Kind Redemption Payments by Hedge Funds: Toward a Fairer Standard. Hirschler Fleischer, a Professional Corporation. Retrieved from: http://www.hf-law.com/news-events/news/in-kind-redemption-payments-by-hedge-funds-toward-a-fairer-standard

Ferri, R. (2014).   REITs And Your Portfolio.   Forbes. Retrieved from: http://www.forbes.com/sites/rickferri/2014/01/07/reits-and-your-portfolio/

Finra, (2015). Putting Too Much Stock in Your Company – A 401(k) Problem. How much is too much?   Financial Industry Regulatory Authority, Inc. Retrieved from: https://www.finra.org/investors/alerts/putting-too-much-stock-your-company_a-401k-problem

Frank, R. (2014, September 22). Billionaires are hoarding piles of cash. Retrieved from CNBC website: http://www.cnbc.com/2014/09/22/billionaires-are-hoarding-piles-of-cash.html

Goldfarb, Z. A. (2010, May 21). SEC launches inquiry into market's 'flash crash'. Washington Post. Retrieved from http://www.washingtonpost.com/wp-dyn/content/article/2010/05/20/AR2010052005086.html

Hallman, G. V. & Rosenbloom, J.S. (2015).   Private Wealth Management. The complete reference for the personal financial planner. (9th ed.). New York. McGraw-Hill Education.

Hathaway, J. (2015). Donald Trump's Grossly Exaggerated Net Worth: A Timeline. Gawker. Retrieved from: http://gawker.com/donald-trumps-grossly-exaggerated-net-worth-a-timeline-1711718182

Investors.com (2015). IBD University. How to Time the Stock Market. Retrieved from: http://education.investors.com/lesson.aspx?id=735751&sourceid=735764

Johnson, B. (2010, November). Powerhouse. Registered Rep, 34(11), 57-62.

Kladec, D. (2014). 22% of workers would rather die early than run out of money. Yet many of the same folks are hardly saving anything for retirement, study finds. Money. Time Inc. Retrieved from: http://time.com/money/3528851/retirement-middle-class-not-saving/

Lavine, A. (2013). MLPs Performing Well. FA Magazine. Charter Financial Publishing Network Inc. Retrieved from: http://www.fa-mag.com/news/mlps-performing-well-13475.html

Livermore, J., & Smitten, R. (2001). How to trade in stocks: The classic formula for understanding timing, money management, and emotional control. New York, NY: McGraw-Hill.

Malkiel, B.G., (2015). A Random Walk Down Wall Street. W. W. Norton & Company, Inc., New York, NY.

Marte, J. (2014). Nearly a quarter of Fortune 500 companies still offer pensions to new hires. The Washington Post. Retrieved from: http://www.washingtonpost.com/news/get-there/wp/2014/09/05/nearly-a-quarter-of-fortune-500-companies-still-offer-pensions-to-new-hires/

McInish, T. & Upson, J. (2015). Financial Markets. Stocks, bonds, money markets; IPOs, auctions, trading (buying and selling), short selling, transaction costs, currencies; futures, options. Vol. 3. U.S.A.

Merrell, S. (2014). Revisiting the lost decade. Retrieved from: http://montereyprivatewealth.com/blog/2014/1/27/revisiting-the-lost-decade

Milken, M. (n.d.) Quotes by Mike Milken: High-yield bonds. Retrieved from http://www.mikemilken.com/quotes.taf

Moroney, R. (2013). Win with consistent income: 4 stocks with 10 years of higher dividends. Forbes. Retrieved from: http://www.forbes.com/sites/gurucentral/2013/09/26/win-with-consistent-income-4-stocks-with-10-years-of-higher-dividends/

Mullaney, T. (2015). A man with an oil bottom bet made for income investors. Data provided by Thomson Reuters. CNBC LLC. Retrieved from: http://www.cnbc.com/2015/03/04/a-man-with-an-oil-bottom-bet-made-for-income-investors.html

Neubert, A. S., Bogle, J. C., Malkiel, B. G. (2013). Indexing for Maximum Investment Results. Routledge Taylor & Francis Group. London and New York.

Patton, M. (2015). Under the Hood: Tax Treatment of ETFs vs. Mutual Funds. ThinkAdvisor. A Summit Professional Networks Website, A division of ALM Media, LLC. Retrieved from: http://www.thinkadvisor.com/2015/03/02/under-the-hood-tax-treatment-of-etfs-vs-mutual-fun?page=2

Pavia, J. (2014). Vested Interest: Rising Rates, Expert Offers key Tips to Handle Rise in Interest Rates, CNBC.com, March 5th 2014, retrieved from: http://www.cnbc.com/id/101452481

PBS. (1995-2010). Frontline: betting on the market. Interview with Jim Cramer. WGBH Educational Foundation. Retrieved from http://www.pbs.org/wgbh/pages/frontline/shows/betting/pros/cramer.html

Philipp, J. (2008). Sales of home safes climb amid financial turmoil. NPR. Retrieved from http://www.npr.org/templates/story/story.php?storyId=95577970

REIT.com, (2015). REITs and Investment Performance. REIT.com. NAREIT's home for all things REIT. Retrieved from: https://www.reit.com/investing/reit-basics/reit-financial-benefits/reits-and-investment-performance

Rotblut, C. & Darst, D. (2012). Using Asset Allocation for Protection and Growth. AAII Journal. June 2012. AAii. Retrieved from: http://www.aaii.com/journal/article/using-asset-allocation-for-protection-and-growth

Rothman, A. (2013). 401(K)s hold risky levels of company stock. CNBC. Retrieved from: http://www.cnbc.com/id/100482094

Rudawsky, G. (2010). Mortgage-backed securities return, but are we really ready? Daily Finance. Retrieved from http://www.dailyfinance.com/story/investing/mortgage-backed-securities-return-but-are-we-really-ready/19452407/

Samaha, L. (2014). Whatever Happened to the Fed Model. Why the so-called Fed model of comparing Treasury yields and the earnings yield on the S&P 500 is not a fail-safe method of valuation. The Motley Fool. Retrieved from: http://www.fool.com/investing/general/2014/01/10/fed-model.aspx

Schlesinger, J. (May 3, 2010). Buffett defends Goldman, Moody's but we still like him. CBS News. Retrieved from http://www.cbsnews.com/8301-503983_162-20003964-503983.html

Schwartz, S.K. (2014). It's time to cash in on dividends. CNBC. Data Provided by Thomson Reuters. Retrieved from: http://www.cnbc.com/2014/01/21/its-time-to-cash-in-on-dividends.html

Seawright B. (2013). Just How Puzzling Are Annuities?, ThinkAdvisor, Retrieved from: http://www.thinkadvisor.com/2013/07/29/just-how-puzzling-are-annuities?page=2

Short, D. (2015). S&P 500 Snapshot: Another Fed Drama. Advisor Perspectives. Advisor Perspectives, Inc. (October 28th, 2015). Retrieved from: http://www.advisorperspectives.com/dshort/updates/Current-Market-Snapshot.php

Slavin, R. (2015). Defaults Reached Record in 2014. The Bond Buyer. SourceMedia. Retrieved from: http://www.bondbuyer.com/news/markets-buy-side/defaults-reached-record-in-2014-1069491-1.html

Smith, R. (2013). Utility Dividends Power Down. Dow Jones & Company, Inc. The Wall Street Journal. Retrieved from: http://www.wsj.com/articles/SB10001424127887323300004578555703569703608

Speth, W. (2015). Beyond BXM & PUT: New Option Strategy Benchmarks. CBOE. Chicago. Retrieved from: http://www.cboe.com/rmc/2015/Day-1-Session-2-Speth.pdf

Spiegeleer, J.D., Schoutens, W., & Van Hulle, C. (2014). The Handbook of Hybrid Securities Convertible bonds CoCo Bonds and Bail-In. West Sussex, United Kingdom. John Wiley & Sons. Ltd.

Stockopedia. (2015). Thomson Reuters, Share Data Services. Price vs. 50 Day Moving Average %. Retrieved from: http://www.stockopedia.com/ratios/price-vs-50-day-moving-average-2/

Voya (2015). Diversify Your Portfolio with Senior Loans. Voya Investments Distributor LLC, New York, NY. Retrieved from: https://investments.voya.com/idc/groups/public/documents/ investor_education/fundspace_bswp-senloan.pdf

Younus, I. (2015). The REIT Industry. CFA Institute Industry Guides. CFA Institute.

Zeng, M. (2015). U.S. 10-year yield hits 2-month low: yield curve flattest since April. Morningstar. Dow Jones Newswires. Dow Jones & Company Inc. Retrieved from: https://www.morningstar. com/news/dow-jones/TDJNDN_2015080310549/us-10year-yield-hits-2month-low-yield-curve-flattest-since-april.html

Zulz, E. (2015). Cash-Heavy Americans are Hurting their Retirement: BlackRock. ThinkAdvisor. Summit Professional Networks, ALM Media. Retrieved from: http://www.thinkadvisor.com/2015/10/26/ cash-heavy-americans-are-hurting-their-retirement?